But I *MEANT* Well!

A STUPID BOOK

ABOUT STUPID THINGS

FOR STUPID PEOPLE

BY A STUPID AUTHOR

by
R.J. NOBLEMAN, Ph.D.

Gotham Books

30 N Gould St.
Ste. 20820, Sheridan, WY 82801
https://gothambooksinc.com/

Phone: 1 (307) 464-7800

© 2024 *R.J. Nobleman, Ph.D*. All rights reserved.

No part of this book may be reproduced, stored in a retrieval system, or transmitted by any means without the written permission of the author.

Published by Gotham Books (July 1, 2024)

ISBN: 979-8-88775-745-2 (H)
ISBN: 979-8-88775-725-4 (P)
ISBN: 979-8-88775-726-1 (E)

Because of the dynamic nature of the Internet, any web addresses or links contained in this book may have changed since publication and may no longer be valid.

The views expressed in this work are solely those of the author and do not necessarily reflect the views of the publisher, and the publisher hereby disclaims any responsibility for them.

Dedicated to

ALVINA
And all the other Basset Hounds of the world,
past, present, and future!

Appreciation is hereby extended to the staff of Gotham Books, Inc., for their encouragement, help, advisement and enthusiasm in the production to this book! For their exceptional assistance and recommendations throughout the entire production process!

TABLE OF CONTENTS

Preface xiii
A Special Note To The Readers Introducing a new literary genre:
"Stupid Books"! xv

PART I. SUBWAY EXPERIENCES

Outsmarted---By A Dog! 1
The Cigarette Smoker Who Would Rather Fight Than Switch! 3
All The News That's Fit To Print! 5
A Visit To The Train Yard 7
A Contagious Laugh Into Hysteria! (or) The No-Laughing Matter That Became A Laughing Matter! 8
Chim Chim-Inee Chim Chim-Inee Chim Chim Cheree, A Sweep Is As Happy As Happy Can Be! 9
Don't Bug Me! 10
"Don't----Don't Shake!" (or) Let's Not Shake, Rattle, and Roll 11
Don't Stare At The Dog! (or) Don't get Rin-Tin-Tin Mad! 13
Ha----Ha! You Got A Tiiiiiiiiiiiiiicket! (or) Boy, Cigarettes Are Sure getting Expensive! 14
His Cup Runneth Under (or) Dreight-me-nisht-in-CUP! 16
Just Follow The Yellow Brick Road! (or) The Ballad of the Munchkins 17
Lop-Sided Bookends (or) The "Tough Guy" That Wasn't So Tough After All! 18
Not Exactly *'Etiquette!* 19
On The Hot Seat! 20
Slap Happy! 22
The Big Horse (or) Mister Ed Speaks 24
You're Not A Sneak-----You're A Snake! (or) Oh my Daaaaaaar-ling... Serpentyne! 25
The Galloping Billboard (or) Images so 'Real' that they 'Jump-Out' at You! 26

Boy, What A Gas! 27

The Chug-A-Lug Dance-A-Thon 28

Miss-----you Broke My Rose! (or) No More 'Flower Power'! 29

PART II. BUSES, CHARTER BUSES, CITY BUSES, MULTI-DAY BUS TOURS

Weeeeeeeeeeeee! It's Better Than Coney Island! 30

The Comedian's Faithful Fan 31

The Paparozzi (or) The Unhappy Neighbor 33

The Hand Is Quicker Than The Eye! (or) Passing the Bar Exam 35

The Bigger They Come, The Harder They Fall! (or) "Heeeeeeey, Do the Mouse Yeah!" 37

The Carnival of Venice (or) Just Whistle While You Ride (The Bus)! (or) Finally, My Chance to Conduct the Band! 38

Splish-Plash I Was Taking A Bath! (or) The Oil Man's Dream: It's A Gusher! 39

"Snap"! 41

Ring The Bell And Run Away! (or) Oops!.... Wrong Number! 42

Poor Bill! 44

On The *Road* It's Ok, But *Here* It's Not Ok??? 46

It Should Happen To You! (or) The Wild Barfer! 47

Help! I've Locked Myself In The Bathroom----And I Can't Get Out! ... 49

Encore! Encore! (or) Tubby the Tuba! 50

Don't Tread On Me! (or) "Put Your Shoe on my Shoooooooouuullllllllder……." 52

Cowboys and Air Conditioners 54

The Case of The "Casokleptomaniac" 55

Look Out Beloooooooooooooow! 57

Hey Kid----Get Out-A- Here! ----Ya Bother Me! 58

Uuuuuuuuh. Errrrrrrrr. Eggggggggg. Agggggggggg. Ehhhhhhh. Irrrrgggggghhh. (or) "Variations in the Language of "Uuuhhh"! 59

The Tree That Was Not There! (or) The Incredible Shrinking Bush (or) The Tree or NOT the Tree! 61

PART III. EXPERIENCES ON AMTRAK AND MULTI-DAY RAIL TRAVEL

"Choo-Choo Chewies" 64

A Spit In Time (But Please, Not On Mine!) 65

The 'Tomato Seed Express' 66

Bigfoot! 67

PART IV. EXPERIENCES ON CRUISE SHIPS, BOATS, FREIGHTER CRUISES, RIVERBOAT CRUISES

A Scene From The Three Stooges (I) (or) An Object in Motion Remains in Motion...... Unless There's a Collision! 68

A Scene From The Three Stooges II 70

"ToooooooooooooooooooooT"! 72

The Cruise From Hell! 75

PART V. EXPERIENCES WITH CARS, CAR SERVICES, TAXI CABS, CAR POOLS, LIMOUSINES, CAR PARKING LOTS

That's Ok, ------My Car Is Big! 80

"Hey Man! This Is New York"! 82

The Guano Entrepreneur (or) This Story Is For The Birds! (or) A Bird In The Air Is Worth Number Two On The Face! 83

In A Pickle (or) The Car with the Swiss Cheese Roof! 85

Doylestown, Pa.----A Nice Place To Visit (But I Wouldn't Want to Try to Hail a Caaaaab There)! 87

The Party Line......In A Taxi Cab???? 88

The "P" 90

Anyone For Chess? 92

Two 'Putzes' 93

PART VI. MY EXPERIENCES ON ELEVATORS

The 'Sabbath' Elevator That Didn't Only Work On The Sabbath! (or) The 'Wanna-Be' Elevator Operator! 95

The *Holy* Elevator (or) The Incident That Happened but Might Not Have Really Happened? 97

"Susan Smith...... Stuck In Elevator". 99

PART VII. FAST-MOVING ANIMALS

The Rider's Turn To Jump 100

Dog Day Morning 102

A Bird In The Cage Is Worth Two On The Floor! 104

PART VIII. THE IMPROMPTU (OR) STORIES THAT REALLY DON'T BELONG IN THIS BOOK, (BUT WHICH I'M ADDING ANYWAY!)

"F-I-R-E" In The Crowded Theatre! 105

There's A Fun-Gus Among-Us! (or) Wild *MUSHROOMS* Couldn't Drive Me Away! 107

No Sense Laughing Over Spilled Milk! 109

Paybacks Are A (son of a) Bitch! (or) Boy, Cigarettes are sure Getting Expensive! 110

Snap, Crackle, Pop! 111

The Laundry Mat From Hell! 112

who Put The "Break" In Bed And Break-Fast? (or) Who Put the Bomp in the Bomp-Ba-Bomp-Ba-Bomp? 113

Why Didn't My Grandparents Like Me? 115

Why Didn't My Grandparents Like Me (II)? (or) Opening Up a Bag of Worms! 116

Wiener-Schnitzel (Pronounced "Veena-Schnitzel") 117

Mmm-Mmm GOOD! (or) Doing the Can-Can (or) The Soup Kitchen 118

PIPE DREAMS (or) The Corn Cob Pipe from Hell! 119

QUIET in the Theatre! (or) The Human BOOMerang! 120

The Happy Juror 121

WIthout Even Thinking! (or) The Case of the 'No-Brainer' 122

Tomato Wars! (or) Like A Scene From 'Animal House'! 123

'BA-DA BOOM' In The Botany Lab!.. 125

Get Out-A-Here Kid Ya' Bother Me (II)! (or) My Audition as a
Replacement for 'Dennis The Menace'!.. 126

Concluding Remarks 1 (or) R.J.'s Final Thought!................................. 128

PART IX. MORE CRAZY STORIES

"We Fell in KAHCKEY!" More Crazy But True Stories.................... 130

Doin' the Bumble Bee Boogie!.. 131

The 'Pizza Rat'!... 132

A Shirt of Many Colors! ("Geeeee, Thannnnnnnks!") 133

"Do You Heff *Elephants* Here??????" 134

The Sun, Grrrrrrrrrrraduation, And 'Big Mike'!................................... 135

"RJ, You Have A *Way* With Birds!" 137

The Malicious, Compulsive Liar! 138

"RJ" -as- "GW" 140

Wahhhhh! Wahhhhhhhh! Wahhhhhhhhhhhhh! I Lost My Coot-sie!!!! 142

Fountain-Pen-Pete ----meets---- Bugger-Nose-Joe!!! 143

Jack in the Box????? No!......Jim In The Box! 144

One Fish, Two Fish......My Fish, You Fish! 145

Why You Should NEVER Keep Keys in Your Shirt Pocket! 146

All Gassed UP! 147

TPP---"The Phart Phone!" 148

Muffled Ears, X2! 149

The LEAST Stupid Teacher! 150

Watch Out For Those 'Robomechanics'! 152

Why You Should NEVER Keep Keys in Your Shirt Pocket! 154

You're Burning The Ceiling!... 155

Let's Fix The Light -----Snap"! 156

Two's Company (Three's Ok Too!)	157
Reservations For Two! (or) "Switch-Tracks"!	158
That's Nothing To Sneeze At!	159
The "Shnorrer"	160
Academy Awaaaaaaaaarrrrrrrd!	161
We're Seeing A Movie!!!?????"	162
"Nobleman Bust His Ass!"	163
Free Guano! (or) Pigeon-Man of Brooklyn!	164
"Put It On The Scale"!	165
The Waffle Iron From Hell!	166
Groucho Duck!	167
"Do You Want To Feel Them?"	168
Coffee Wars	169
The Dripping Wet Umbreela!	171
I Don't Know!!!!!!!	172
Pica-Dilly-Dilly!	173
Crabapples!!!	174
"Ladies And Gentlemen……, Lend Me Your Ears"! ---- "Owwwwwwwww!!!"	175
Fried Fish------------You Put It In A Dish!	176
"Roast Puffin and Walrus Liver"!	178
The Fish That Died!	179
The 'Zhlubbb' Factor!	180
2-2-Loo To Too-Too-Loo!	181
Re-Stocking The Sewer!	182
"Mr. Clothes-Pin"!	183
A Question About The Squirrels!	184
The Disappearing Act!	185
There's A Face In My Soup!	186
The Mystery Of The Garnished Cigarette!	188

Give It To The Cat!...189

How I Invented The "Selfie"!..190

Be Careful What You Wear!..191

"My Grandmother Did It!"..192

"Well…They Gotta Eat Too!"..193

"Oh! What A Tangled Web (Fishing Line) We Weave!"......................194

A Real 'Dennis The Menace'! ---or--- The Return of The Pest!..........195

Roller Derby! ---or--- Becoming The Chair-Man!................................196

The Horse That "Don't Look Too Good Today"!..................................197

"Oh-Shit!!! Oh-Shit!!! Nobleman's Talking To A Piece of Chalk!!!".198

"Shut-Uuuuuupppppppppppppp!"...199

Good, But A Bit Too 'Peppery'!..200

The Squirrels Are Coming! The Squirrels Are Coming!.....................201

Wild Goose Chase!..202

How I Deal With 'Nuisance' Calls: Telemarketers, Robo-Callers, And Scammers!...203

Boooooooooom!...205

The Fortune Cookie From Hell!...206

"Uh-Uh-Uh-Uh-Uh-Uh-Uh-Uh-Uh-Uh-Uh-Uh-Uh-Uh-Uh-Uh-Uh"!!!208

"You Made Me Lose My Fly????----Whammmmmmm!!!"..................209

The Obscene Phone Call That Wasn't!..210

The Snowstorm In May!..211

Look Out Beloooooooooooooow!...212

Cane And Able!-or-When It Comes To Using A Cane, Am I Able????
....213

Two Left Feet!...214

Picture Perfect!...215

Sometimes, It Pays To Procrastinate!..216

In The Wine-Making (or 'Glass-Blowing') Business!..........................217

No Microscopes Today!..218

x

I Did That Purposely!!!!!	219
Professors From Hell!	221
"Food Fiiiiiiiiiiiiiiiight!!!"	224
Musical Chairs (Without The Music)!	226
"Mom, Dad…...Did You Know That My Shoes Crawled Under The Radiator, And RJ Was On *Television* !!!!	228
Doin' The Peach Pit (W)Rap)!	229
No Sense Crying Over Spilled Water! (or) Her Glass Runneth Over!	230
Can We Pleeeeease Get The Vocalist Out of Here!!!	231
Washing-Machine Blues!	233
"Only The Nose Knows!"	235
Jumpin' In Da 'Hood'! ------(or)---- Who's Been Jumping In Myyyyy Hood?	237
RJ, You Have A *Way* With Birds!"	239
The Malicious, Compulsive Liar!	240
The Sun, Grrrrrrrrrrraduation, And 'Big Mike'!	242
A Shirt of Many Colors! (Geeeee, Thannnnnnnks!")	244
"RJ----Can You Please Go Outside and Find Out Why The Baby's Crying?"	245
Y'ah Poooooop!	246
Cat On A Hot Tin Motor!	247
No Free Coffee!	248
"Instant Shmuck Identification!"	249
"Thank You For Playing The Trombone" Brought to You By The Principal From Hell!	250
Chim Chiminey, Chim Chiminey, And The 'Genius' Next Door!	253
The "Bear-Inarian"!	255
Skunks Awaaaaaaaay!	257
"Banquet?????……*What* Banquet?????"	258
"RJ, Haven't You Had Enough?"	260

"Z-Z-Z-Z-Z-Z-Z-Z-Z"! -or- Trying To Be Rip Van Winkle (In Class)! 261
Mrs. Sharp-Rock! 263
The Kid Who Refused To Handle The Rock 265
"RJ---I Think It's Time For You To Get Another Degree!" 267
"And Me And All My Papers Got Soaking Wet!!!" 268
The Case of The Missing Master's Degree! 269
The RJ Appleseed Game! 271
"Bingo!!!" 273
"Echyl-Bah-Dechyl!" 274
The Carbon Monoxide Detector From Hell! 275
The Bakery From Hell 277
Why You Should *Never* Chew Gum In Class! 278
"Ohhhhhhhhh! Dissin' The Teacher's Onions!" 280
Burning Aces'! 281
The Movie Projector--------From Hell! 283
"Well, Now That Somebody's Here, I Guess I'll Have To Wash My Hands!" 285
Who's That Tap-Ping, At My Shoul-Der? 286
"An Old Bag!" 288
Day Camp Sonatas! 290
"Make Sure You Eat The Cream!" 292
"rrrrrrrrrrrrrrRIPPPPPPPP!" and 'Spider Man'! 293
The Orange Conspiracy! 295
"You Might As Well Hand Out Popcorn"! 297
Left with Egg On Her Face! 298
Concluding Remarks 2 299

Preface

When I told a friend of mine that I was planning to write a book about the crazy things I've seen on the New York City subways, he paused for a second., then turned around and said, "Ya know---that's something that probably EVERYBODY who lives in New York can write a book about"! Thinking about that, I guess he was right! I'm sure that everyone whom has ridden the New York City subways has seen some crazy, outrageous things! A father of another friend of mine told me that he rides the subways every day, at all different hours, and "you wouldn't BELIEVE some of the nuts I see!"

Anyway, as I started to write the book, I realized that not only have I seen crazy things on the subways, I've seen plenty of crazy things on buses too. So I thought I should I should those stories as well.

As I continued writing, I realized that plenty of crazy things have also happened on other modes of transportation as well: tour buses, car services and taxis, car pools, big cruise ships, small cruise ships, AMTRAK, --- on basically any mode of transportation that I've used, I've witnessed or have been involved in some outrageous incidents that to *me* were funny, even if some others don't think they're funny, so I've included those stories as well. When people have asked me why I'm throwing in all kinds of stories from all other modes of transportation if the book was originally limited to subways, I tell them a motto or policy that I learned from my high school music teacher. Whenever anyone questioned the way he did certain things, or why he did them, he would say:" I'm the BOSS here! I give the ORDERS! I call the SHOTS! The TAIL does not wag the DOG!" I used to love hearing him say that, because every time he did so, I would wonder what it would look like to see a tail wagging its DOG! I would try to form a picture in my mind of a tail standing still, with the DOG wagging back and forth! (Come to think of it, suppose someone had a bulldog, or Doberman, or boxer, ----dogs whose tails are usually clipped shortly after birth----would you see a dog wagging all by itself, WITHOUT the tail?). What would THAT look like?

You may be wondering why, of all the forms of transportation I've included, there's no mention of airline travel. That's because I don't travel by air---I guess you can say I've got "flyophobia"! But if I did travel by air, I'm SURE I would have stories about that too!

Finally, the last section in this book is entitled "The Impromptu". In that section, I threw in stories that are funny (at least in MY opinion) but which have NOTHING to do, WHATSOEVER, with transportation or travel, but which I felt I would like to add. You may ask why I would put such stories into this book. The answer is the same as I previously explained: "It's MY book, I'm the BOSS here………. the TAIL does not wag the DOG!".

Finally, I would like to mention that the stories told here are all TRUE! They really HAPPENED! MY intention here is not to degrade nor "dis" the NYC subway system, AMTRAK, cruise lines, bus companies, taxis, etc.; I'm just reporting on what I actually saw, heard, felt, and experienced! Now, sit back, and ENJOY! I also hope you can deal with my obnoxiousness which periodically raises up its arrogant head in many of the stories!

Brooklyn, New York
January, 2024
R.J. Nobleman

A SPECIAL NOTE TO THE READERS
Introducing a new literary genre: "STUPID BOOKS"!

The book you are about to enjoy is non-fiction—all stories are true! The genre is comedy or humor, but it is a very special type of humor, namely, STUPIDITY! I have several college/university degrees, being a 'professional student', but my uncle Izzy always told me that he felt all that college wasn't necessary, and that I should think about getting another degree, in "STUPIDITY"! After thinking that over, I decided I should not only write a book on STUPIDITY, but I should create an entirely new literary genre (an offset of humor): "STUPIDITY"! So this book is a benchmark book in that new genre! It describes all sorts of STUPID things I did when I was a kid, or things that I witnessed. Many of these STUPID incidents occurred on the NYC subways and buses. Other things occurred in all other fields.

As you can infer from reading, when I was a kid, I was a real "Dennis the Menace"! I probably still am! However, these acts of stupidity were not done intentionally; they were usually done out of fun or just plain unintentionally. That's the reason for the title "BUT I MEANT WELL"! I'm sure all of you did STUPID things when you were a kid also (and most of you probably STILL do some STUPID things as an adult! I suggest that after every short story you read here, you say to yourself "BUT I MEANT WELL!" or "BUT HE MEANT WELL", or, "BUT RJ MEANT WELL!". I'm sure most, if not all of you, can each write your OWN book about STUPID things you've done or seen throughout your life (but were afraid or embarrassed to admit)! Anyway, from now on, any time you see or do anything STUPID, you should realize first that it was STUPID, then say to yourself "BUT I MEANT WELL!".

Brooklyn, New York
January, 2024
R.J. Nobleman

PART I. SUBWAY EXPERIENCES

OUTSMARTED---BY A DOG!

I was on my way home from work one day in the early 90's, standing on the platform of the A train in Queens. This is an elevated line, and one of the LEAST things I would expect to see is a DOG walking on the platform! Yet, right before my eyes, a German Shepherd suddenly appears! How he got there, or when, or by whom, is an unsolved mystery, yet the reality was that he was there and I perceived a dangerous situation for him. He could, theoretically, fall off the platform and break a leg, or fall down to the street below—about a fifty foot drop, or he could get hit by a train! I realized that I HAD to get him off the platform and OFF the train station! I had to do this even if it meant I would have to exit the station, get him off, and return by paying another fare. I realized the streets would not be the safest place for a stray dog either, but he would be safer THERE than on the platform! So I kept calling him" here boy, here boy", and whistling, and patting my thigh. He just paused and looked at me, as if he couldn't decide whether to follow me or ignore me altogether. After about ten minutes of my coaxing him to follow me down the stairs and off the platform, a train was pulling into the station! Then I knew that time was CRUCIAL! I had to somehow convince this dog to follow me off the platform! As the train pulled into the station and the doors were about to open, I FRANTICALLY continued to beckon him off---"here boy, here boy, here boy" I kept saying, whistling, patting my thigh—to no avail! The train doors opened and the passengers were watching me frantically calling that dog! Again he paused, looked me in the face, turned, and walked right into the subway car! He turned around again, looked me in the face, and watched as the doors closed. The train started to pull out of the station, and the passengers were HYSTERICAL!, pointing and laughing at me on the platform while the dog was on the train! Maybe they thought it was MY dog??? I felt maaaaad stupid standing there—the dog was on the train, I was still on the platform!

Later on that evening my friend came over to visit. He came by quite often since we liked to sit around and 'throw the bull'. I told him the story, and he laughed just as hard as the passengers did that day! "Ah-HA-HA-HA-HA" he said! "Outsmarted by a DOG!"

"Ph.D."! "DOCTOR'S DEGREE"! "Outsmarted by a DOG!" "Ah-HA-HA-HA-HA…...!"

THE CIGARETTE SMOKER WHO WOULD RATHER FIGHT THAN SWITCH!

It was in July, 1983; I was on the F train headed towards downtown Brooklyn to work at a special, unpaid, internship program. It was a little after 9 AM, still considered the "rush hour", but near the end of it. The trains were still fairly crowded---some seats still available, but relatively few. Some passengers were standing (straphangers). All of a sudden, one of the standing passengers, leaning against the train doors, decided it was time for a smoke. Smoking is illegal in the subways, even back then, but some people who are brazen or just plain stupid still do it, every now and then. It's just too bad they don't get caught too often! I'm not trying to 'DIS' smokers here, because I'm a smoker myself (cigars)!

After he 'lit up' one guy, a passenger seated not far away from him politely asked him to put the cigarette out, but the smoker just kind of ignored him. Then another passenger, a younger guy, decided he was going to show off his 'macho' image, and he asked the guy once, then twice more, to put out the cigarette. The smoker began to curse in another language, yelling and screaming---I couldn't make out every word, but basically telling him to shut his mouth because he wasn't a cop! This scenario went on for about 10 minutes, with the smoker SCREAMING at the top of his lungs (no pun intended)! Other passengers, (typical New Yorkers—myself included), as usual, pulled a 'Sergeant Schultz" and made believe nothing was going on ("I saw no-thing…...NO-THING!"). The guy who originally asked the smoker to put out the cigarette, was quiet—kind of apologetic----and asked the 'macho' guy to just forget the whole thing—let the guy smoke and hope he BURNS----not to push this crazy smoking lunatic over the edge! Understanding the language of the smoker, somewhat, however,

I heard him say something to the 'macho' guy like "…at the next station, we are going to FIGHT"! Some of the passengers began to laugh, even to joke with each other. I think they were excited about the chance of seeing a fight! Well, at the next station, Jay Street, the smoker and the 'macho' guy got off the train, but so did almost everyone else (this station is a major junction and transfer stop). What actually happened after that I do not know. I was late (as usual) and didn't have time to stick around. So many passengers got off the train at that station that chances are the lunatic smoker and 'macho' guy lost each other in the shuffle. So…. did they fight or didn't they fight? To this very day, THAT is the QUESTION!

ALL THE NEWS THAT'S FIT TO PRINT!

I was walking on an underground subway platform in midtown Manhattan, I think it was on 42nd Street and Eighth Avenue. As I passed by a staircase, I noticed a bunch of teens were hanging out at the top. You could see they were just looking for trouble, real 'wanna-be' juvenile delinquents waiting to be 'sworn-in'! They were making all kinds of noise, yelling, screaming, laughing, cursing—just waiting for a mischievous opportunity to come their way! A bunch of real, future, *Bona Fide* hoodlums and low-lives! (I'm sorry I can't think of a more realistic description)! I'd say they were in their late teens or possibly early twenties—probably about five or six of them. One did not have to be a rocket scientist to see that those BUMS had no lives of their own, that they were only out to cause misery to others, just for the sake of getting their 'kicks'! (Boy, would I have loved to give them a few KICKS!).

Anyway, it was a hot summer day, and I was walking along the platform, slowly, waiting for the train. As I passed by the staircase, one of those morons decided to throw a newspaper down the staircase, at me (he probably had no use for the newspaper anyway, since you have to be LITERATE to read it)! I guess for him, that was his way of getting his 'kicks'—to have the newspaper land on top of me! As the newspaper fell, it opened, and pages came apart and went flying all over the place! It so happened that one of the sheets of newspaper reached its 'target' and landed on my head, covering my entire head and most of my face. Any other person probably would have grabbed the paper, crumbled it up, thrown it on the floor, and probably would have cursed that lowlife S.O.B. out either out loud or under his breath, BUT NOT ME! What did I do??? I saw that as an opportunity to get a LAUGH (from someone else). I didn't care WHO laughed—wouldn't matter if it were ME, some other passengers, or even those lowlife bastards themselves—so long as SOMEONE got a laugh out of it! So what I did was to continue walking along the platform, slowly, at the same pace, wearing my new newspaper 'bonnet' over my head, as if I were totally OBLIVIOUS to the whole incident! With my entire head and part of my face covered by the one sheet of newspaper, I continued my stroll along the subway platform as if nothing had happened, at least for a few minutes, until I passed the staircase completely! And, of course, I heard those MORONS laughing, not because they hit their 'target', but because of my obliviousness—walking with my new newspaper 'bonnet' over my head! (Maybe I should have saved it for the next Easter parade!).

I guess that shows that I will do just about ANYTHING for a laugh, even if the only laughs I get come from lowlife slime balls!

A VISIT TO THE TRAIN YARD

I always wondered what a trip to the train yard would be like. Imagine, seeing all those trains—hundreds and hundreds—maybe even thousands of subway cars lined up end to end, standing there with their motors shut down until they are needed. Well, one day, my wish came true, although I wasn't too thrilled about it! I was on my way to work as a teacher, and had to be there by a certain time. I was on the "A" train at Euclid Avenue in Brooklyn, where there are two tracks that can be used to get into Queens (where I had to go). When we arrived at the Euclid Avenue station, there was already a train on the other track, and nobody seemed to know which train would pull out first. Suddenly, an announcement was made over the loudspeaker "the train on the side track will be leaving first; the train on the center track is going into the train yard". Obviously, I had no choice but to get onto the train on the side track; not only was it going to pull out first, but the other train that I was on (in the center track) was going into the train yard!

Apparently, the 'geniuses' who run the system intended the train on the side track to go into Queens, but it didn't quite work out that way! It seemed to be taking a longer time than usual to get to the next station, and I didn't seem to recognize the landscape as it was traveling. As you can probably, guess, they sent my train into the train yard instead, by accident! All the train workers who saw a train coming into the train yard full of passengers realized what happened, and they were laughing hysterically! I was pissed because this meant I would be late to work, because I had to wait for those 'geniuses' to back the train out of the yard and return it to the Euclid Avenue station, where I had to wait for the next train! Sometimes you have to be careful what you wish for---it may come true!

A CONTAGIOUS LAUGH INTO HYSTERIA! (or) The No-Laughing Matter That Became A Laughing Matter!

I was sitting in a subway car one day and very few passengers were present. On the seats opposite me were a few young women who obviously knew each other. Suddenly one of them started smiling at one of the others as if something funny was going on, although nobody seemed to know WHAT. Then the others started grinning as well, but one at a time, then they all started grinning at each other for no apparent reason. I was sitting opposite them and watching all this ensue and that caused ME to start to grin! This grinning between them back and forth and between them and me back and forth went on for about fifteen minutes, like a snowball effect! We were all grinning and laughing silently although nobody seemed to know what the hell it was all about! Anyway, when my station arrived and I got up to exit the train, they waved at me and continued to grin!

CHIM CHIM-INEE CHIM CHIM-INEE CHIM CHIM CHEREE, A SWEEP IS AS HAPPY AS HAPPY CAN BE!

After traveling underground from Manhattan to Brooklyn, the "N" Line (called the "Sea Beach") runs above ground from 8th Avenue to Coney Island. As it travels on the surface, it crisscrosses many streets and avenues where both cars and people walk on the overpasses above. At these spots, overpass bridges exist and pedestrians can watch from above as the trains pass below. Several years ago, before the newest trains were built, the 'old' subway cars had cheese-cloth-like gratings on their ceilings (probably for ventilation). Anyhow, kids (actually 'punks'—most likely future juvenile delinquents, if not ALREADY menaces to society) on these overpasses sometimes threw stones onto the tops of the subway cars as they passed below, probably for 'kicks"! When the stones hit the roofs of the subway cars, they would bounce off, but INSIDE the car, a mass of black SOOT would fall out of the gratings on the ceilings of the subway cars. Anyone who was unlucky enough, I guess by negative 'serendipity', to be standing directly below that area of the grating system inside the car (where the stone hit the roof) immediately became covered with SOOT! In an instant they changed careers, and became chimney sweeps!

DON'T BUG ME!

I was on the subway that was not yet traveling underground. Many stations are on the street surface, and many are elevated as well. This train was on street level. When the doors opened at one station, a giant bug—some kind of dragon fly or possibly a locust or cicada—entered the car and started flying around all over the place. People, men and women, were running away from it and screaming. It kept flying back and forth terrorizing everybody. Finally, when the train got to the next station and the doors opened, the bug flew out, and everyone gave a sigh of relief and then laughed about the entire incident. Obviously, we were all glad it was over---or so we THOUGHT! The doors remained open at the station for about an extra half-minute or so, and, suddenly, the big bug flew back in! The same scenario ensued, but luckily, before the doors closed again, it flew back out!

"DON'T----DON'T SHAKE!" (or) Let's Not Shake, Rattle, and Roll

When I was in college, I used to work part-time for a tobacco company in Manhattan. On days when I had no classes, I would go to work from my home using the subway, but on days where I had only one or two classes, or several hours between classes, I used to go back and forth—to school, then to work, then back to school, back to work, all by subway.

Anyway, at the station near the college there was an ice cream store, and students would often buy cones, sundaes, and shakes, and bring them onto the trains. I often bought a shake and brought it onto the train. Well, the station was actually the last stop of the subway line, so in general, when you entered the station, there was a train already there with its doors open ready for boarding. The task was to board the train BEFORE it closed its doors! Once the doors closed, you would have to wait for the next train to enter the station, and it could take another ten or fifteen minutes before that train entered and pulled back out. So if one was in a hurry---like I was---to get back to work, you'd better be quick about getting into a train that still had its doors open!

Anyway, one day I was about to board a train, as its doors were still open. I had my shake with my, but for whatever reason I threw away its cover. Just as I was about to board, the doors began to close. I HAD to get on THAT train, in order to get to work, or I would be delayed by fifteen more minutes, and time is money! So as I was entering hastily with the doors closing, the shake started to spill and splatter! There was a guy sitting on the seat close to the doors who was afraid that the shake would splatter on HIM! So he waved his arms in the air at me and said, in a panic,

"DON'T-----DON'T SHAKE!!!----they'll open the DOORS again!!!----they'll open the DOORS again!!!"

Finally they did open the doors again, and I entered peacefully---you should have heard the sigh and the look of RELIEF on the guy's face!

DON'T STARE AT THE DOG! (or)
Don't get Rin-Tin-Tin Mad!

I was on the subway one night, when a cop with a canine companion/police dog entered the train. He and the dog were on patrol, standing near the car doors. A kid (teen low-life) sitting near me was looking at the dog, and the dog looked back at him. The kid deliberately started to stare at the dog, and you could see from the expression on the dog's face that he was getting mad! The cop warned the kid "Don't stare at the dog!" "You stare that DOG down and you'll deserve everything that you're gonna get"! Interpretation: the dog will tear his ass up and he (the cop) will LET him! Result: the kid quickly stopped staring at the dog!

HA----HA! YOU GOT A Tiiiiiiiiiiiiiicket! (or) Boy, Cigarettes Are Sure getting Expensive!

I was riding on the F train in Queens one night, it was probably about 10 PM, the train was nearly empty, and the car I was in had only about 4 or 5 passengers. Two teenage boys were sitting together, and one of the felt it was time to 'light-up' (a cigarette). Before lighting-up, he looked around the car carefully to make sure no cops were present., then he moved into a corner seat, so as not to be seen easily, and started to enjoy his cigarette. WHO walks in very slowly and 'suavely' at the next stop??? A COP! He sees the kid smoking and immediately begins writing him out a ticket! The kid kept saying he was "sorry", yada, yada, yada, and begins making all kinds of excuses, even claiming that he didn't know it was illegal to smoke on the subway! But the cop couldn't care less! He was getting ENJOYMENT out of writing the ticket! And I was getting enjoyment out of watching the whole scenario! GOOD for the BASTARD! When he lit-up he couldn't care less if the smoke bothered anyone else! Now it was payback time! You should have seen the look on the guy's face! Boy…. was he PISSED on getting a ticket! I had the urge to burst out laughing and say "HA-HA…. you got a tiiiiiiiiicket!", but of course, I didn't. I pulled a "Sergeant Shultz"---"I saw no-thing, NO-THING!" I was thinking of waiting until they both got off the train, and as soon as the doors would close, I would point at them and LAUGH, HYSTERICALLY! But then, I thought, with MY luck, the doors would probably open again, and I would be in MAAAAAAAD trouble! And even if the doors would not have opened again, I might find myself in the same subway car with them some night in the future---then they might recognize me, and I would have to deny knowing anything about it; I might even have to claim that I couldn't speak English! So, anyway, I decided not to do it, but will always wish I COULD have done it! I guess I'm showing the 'obnoxious' streak in me!

HIS CUP RUNNETH UNDER (or)
Dreight-me-nisht-in-CUP!

I was waiting on the subway platform for a train one night in mid-summer. One of the station attendants was sweeping and emptying the trash receptacles. All of a sudden, this guy appears; he was about 20 years old, wearing an under-shirt, and starts SCREAMING at the station attendant, "you THREW AWAY MY CUP MAN, you THREW AWAY MY CUP!!!" I wasn't sure what that was all about, but from what I could surmise, this guy must have had a coffee or soda container, and he must have placed it down on the floor or something, and walked away for a few seconds; when the attendant passed by, he saw the cup, thought it was someone's trash, and threw it in the trash container. It's hard to imagine that someone would go 'bananas' over a paper coffee cup, but he did!

The guy continued to yell and scream at the attendant, who yelled and screamed back, telling the guy that if you leave something on the platform, or if he sees what looks like trash laying around that doesn't belong to anyone, that it's his JOB to throw it away! The screaming match ensued anyway, and the attendant told the guy to stay put while he gets a cop! As the attendant walked up the staircase to get a cop (as if you would really *find* one when you need one!), the coffee cup guy smacks the attendant on the ass! Then the coffee cup guy must have gotten cold feet, figuring a cop would have arrested him, so he walked away! In Yiddish I believe that "cup" means "head" or "head and the brains inside". This 'coffee cup guy' certainly was not using his "cup"!

JUST FOLLOW THE YELLOW BRICK ROAD! (or)
The Ballad of the Munchkins

It was a warm summer day, and my friend and I visited Coney Island for a few hours. We entered the subway station at the Coney Island terminal, which is named Stillwell Avenue. That is the last stop in Brooklyn. Several different subway lines begin and end there, such as the N,F,W, and D, among others. I don't remember the reason, but several subway lines were re-routed that day, so the passengers had to walk up and down several different staircases and platforms to get to the line they needed. With hundreds of passengers going through that 'maze', the place looked like some kind of PARADE was going on! Several subway workers were on their break, and they were standing around watching this 'parade' of passengers. One of them, as he was watching this 'parade' began to sing his favorite song, which was appropriate for the occasion, from the Wizard of Oz "follow the yellow brick road.... follow the yellow brick road......follow-follow-follow-follow-FOLLOW THE YELLOW BRICK ROAD!" He continued to sing this favorite song, but what made it worse was that since this song was sung in the movie by the Munchkins, he sang the song just like a MUNCHKIN! (Personally, I didn't think he would do too well on American Idol!). My friend turned to me and said "THAT'S what's running our trains"!

LOP-SIDED BOOKENDS (or)
The "Tough Guy" that wasn't so tough after all!

I was sitting on a subway seat, a seat which can hold two, or, at most, three average-sized people. Another passenger was sitting on the other end. A few minutes later, another passenger enters the train—a big, tall guy, with a paperback book in his hand, and squeezes in-between us, continuing to read his paperback. When he sat down, it was a really tight squeeze, but he sat his ass down anyway, reading his paperback, oblivious to the fact that he caused all three of us to feel like sardines in a can. Didn't even say "excuse me" ----couldn't care less about the problem he just caused! A few seconds later, the other passenger who was seated at the other end of the seat told him that he should have said "excuse me". The guy with the paperback then replied "what are you---TOUGH guy?". What ensued was yelling and screaming between those two---I just sat there making believe I knew nothing about anything! I thought the paperback guy was going to get hit, because the other guy was screaming louder and louder: "you're supposed to say excuse me, EXCUSE me!" Suddenly the paperback guy wasn't so 'tough' anymore! "OK chill, …. CHILL" the paperback guy kept saying, and he got off the train at the next stop! Sometimes, the bigger they come, the harder they fall!

NOT EXACTLY *'ETIQUETTE!*

I was on a subway car and seated opposite me was a guy eating some take-out Chinese food from a Styrofoam container. Apparently, there were some things in the food that he did not like because he was throwing them away. The question here is WHERE was he throwing them AWAY???? On the floor, of course! Where ELSE??? He ate the food with a fork and spoon, and after every five or so mouthfuls, he would simply use the fork to throw away whatever he didn't want, right onto the floor! I just sat there and, like almost everyone else, just made believe I saw NOTHING! (or, as Sergeant Schultz would say, I see no-thing, NO-THING)!

ON THE HOT SEAT!

While riding on a train one night, a man, his wife, and child sat on the seats opposite me. Before they sat down, there was already a man sitting there (actually SLEEPING, and totally out-of-it!). This guy was completely OUT, somewhere in 'Never-Never Land', he wouldn't nor couldn't wake up for anything! (I'll call him "Rip Van Winkle"!)

The situation was rather uneventful for about five or ten minutes, when suddenly Rip Van Winkle's head falls on the other guy's shoulder. Things like this happen all the time on a train; someone dozes off and their head tilts onto the next person's shoulder. Often, as the sleeper's head tilts, the angle automatically wakes him up and he apologizes (sometimes) and straightens up. This time, however, that didn't happen. Van Winkle's head rested on the other guy's shoulder as if it were a pillow!

"Hey man---get your head off my arm", the other guy yells. But Rip Van Winkle didn't (and couldn't) budge! He was totally out-of-it! The man continued to scream this again and again at Van Winkle, getting louder and louder and madder and madder! But Rip Van Winkle didn't budge! Then the man told his wife and kid to find other seats, because : "I'm going to DECK this guy!" I suspected that meant he was going to punch him. He repeated this over and over, but Van Winkle didn't (and couldn't) budge! Finally, it looked like the guy was about to 'DECK' him, but at the last second, he said "Naaaah, I can't DECK nobody when they're sleeping". At that point he arrived at (in HIS mind) a better solution. He took out his cigarette lighter, rolled up some newspaper (which he got from the ones previous passengers leave on their seats) and set them on fire! He then said "I'm gonna BURN this guy's ASS", and threw the burning newspapers right on the seat where Van Winkle was sitting (sleeping), and moved out of the way! But Van Winkle was still totally out-of-it! Other passengers then began to yell to Van Winkle

"HEY, GET UP, GET UP, You'll catch on FIRE!" But Van Winkle was still completely out-of-it! Finally, another passenger (the "hero") came over and kicked the burning papers to the floor and stomped out the fire before Rip Van Winkle got burned.

You should have seen the LOOK the man who set the papers on fire gave the "hero", as if to say "Hey man, how DARE you put out my fire!" I thought the man and the "hero" were going to fight, but the man, his wife and kid got off a couple of stations later.

As for Rip Van Winkle, I don't know WHEN he finally woke up, but I'm sure that by now his twenty years is finally up!

SLAP HAPPY!

It was the summer of 1977. Everyone in New York was paranoid about who the Son of Sam actually was, and when and where would the next strike! People were reporting anyone and everyone who looked or acted suspicious to the police. I have a friend who was interrogated by the police as a potential suspect, obviously reported to them by an enemy of his! This friend of mine was actually afraid of his own shadow, so the fact that HE was reported to them was outrageous! My point here is that ANYONE who acted insane or even a bit abnormal was suspect, and often reported to the police.

I entered the subway and found a seat. The car was relatively crowded but there were some seats available. Sitting directly opposite me was a woman with her two young sons, probably aged 6 and 7. Boys will be boys, and these two were no exception. They were both facing backward in their seats, looking out the train window (the train was still above ground at that point). Anyway, one kid decided to smack the other in the back of his head while they were both looking out the window, and then to make believe HE did not do it! Then, the kid that got smacked returned the favor, smacking the first kid in the back of the head and making believe HE did not do it. This made me laugh, because it reminded me of The Three Stooges, my favorites! Then the first kid did it again, smacking his brother in the back of the head, and the brother reciprocated, smacking HIM in the back of the head again! This made me laugh even more! This scenario continued for about ten minutes, causing me to become HYSTERICAL! It seems that the more I laughed, the more they did it! Finally, I became so hysterical in my seat, that I couldn't STAND it anymore! I decided that I had to get away from those guys, because I was laughing so hard I couldn't even catch my breath! So I got up and walked to the other end of the car, but I was laughing hysterically as I walked! Finally, I saw an empty seat all the way at the end of the car, and I sat down, still laughing hysterically! Opposite me there was a young woman seated, who had no idea as to what I had just experienced. When she saw me sit down, hysterical, you should have seen the look of FEAR on her face! She probably thought I was a LUNATIC—maybe even the Son of Sam himself! Just then the train pulled in to the next station—she jumped up and ran off the train! I wanted to yell out to her, explaining that I wasn't crazy, ---that I was laughing because of what I had just seen at the other end of the car—but it was too late---she was GONE!

THE BIG HORSE (or) Mister Ed Speaks

When the subways are crowded, almost everyone scrambles for an empty seat. Sometimes you get 'squished' even if you have a seat, especially if the person or persons sitting beside you are 'extra large'! One day this woman must have felt squished, because the guy sitting beside her was "extra large". When the car began to empty she told him that he should have found another empty seat, so there would be more room for her and other passengers. He asked her why SHE didn't look for another seat, and what the problem was with both of them remaining where they were sitting. She told him that she felt "squished", because he was "a big horse"! They continued to argue, and she repeated, a couple of times "you're a big HORSE…... you're a big HORSE!" Apparently someone at the other end of the car overheard them, and started 'whinnying': "WEEEEE-HEEE-HEEEE-HEEEE-HEEEEEEEEE,…… WEEEEEE-HEEEEE-HEEEE-HEEEEE-HEEEE"!

YOU'RE NOT A SNEAK-----YOU'RE A SNAKE! (or)
Oh my Daaaaaaar-ling... Serpentyne!

I was riding home one night on the F train, and it was fairly crowded. I wouldn't say there was 'standing room only', but most of the seats were filled. So this young woman, probably in her early twenties, sits next to me, and everything is going *status quo,*---yada, yada, yada. As we're riding, **something,**---I don't know exactly WHAT---tells me to look down towards my side—at the boundary between us. Maybe I thought I felt something strange, like something had brushed against me---I'm not exactly sure. So I looked, and what did I see??? There was a BOA CONSTRICTOR wrapped around her body! Not wanting to show fear, I just continued to sit there and make believe I really hadn't seen ANYTHING (like Sergeant Schultz---I saw no-thing...., NO-THING!) I figured that maybe if I didn't look again, maybe it would go away...or maybe it wasn't really there at ALL---that I was just IMAGINING the whole thing! She got off a few stops later,---that is—her and her figment of my IMAGINATION! I just continued to sit there non-chilauntly, making believe the whole thing never really happened!

THE GALLOPING BILLBOARD (or) Images so 'Real' that they 'Jump-Out' at You!

On most subway stations, there are giant subway maps/signs placed throughout the stations. These maps show all the subway lines throughout the city. They show all the stations that the trains stop at, and where transfers can be made from one train line to another. The maps are huge, usually about four or five feet high by three or four feet wide, approximately. Sometimes these signs show various advertisements in addition to or instead of subway maps. One day a young woman was looking at one of the maps very carefully. She was probably trying to figure out which trains would take her to her destination and what stations she would need to get to in order to make the necessary transfers. What she did NOT know, however, was that on the opposite side of the map, two kids—teens—were horsing around, pushing and shoving each other. As she was looking at the map, on the other side, one kid pushed another into the sign, and the map suddenly got PUSHED toward her! You should have seen the look of FEAR on her face—for the split second that this happened! Imaging looking at a sign and it suddenly POPS OUT at you! As I saw this unfold, of course, I became HYSTERICAL! When she realized what actually happened, she also laughed. I hope she doesn't have nightmares!

BOY, WHAT A GAS!

I was on a crowded subway car, during the rush hour. As is typical for that hour, the trains are MAD crowded! Standing room only, and usually everybody's packed like a sardine can! Anyway, there was a handicapped guy standing amongst us, and he apparently had to pass some gas. All of a sudden, we hear "PFFFFFFFFFFTTTT"!

People began looking at each other and holding their noses! Some farts don't smell, but this one sure as hell DID!!! Well, I guess if anyone had nasal congestion that day, it sure cleared up!

THE CHUG-A-LUG DANCE-A-THON

I was waiting for a train on a Saturday morning to get to a class I was taking at a college in lower Manhattan. The class started at 9:00, but with my tardy self, it was almost 8:30 already, and if I were only one-half hour late, it would be good (at least for me).

Of course, I had to wait mad long for a train; when one finally arrived, it passed right by, without stopping! On the back deck of the last car of that train, two guys were dancing back and forth (but there wasn't even any music!). What the hell THAT was all about was beyond me!

I went downstairs to the token booth clerk and asked him why that train just passed us by, without stopping, and he mumbled some kind of 'gibberish' answer! I asked him the same question again, and he mumbled the same 'gibberish' response again! To this day, I still don't know what that was all about! My guess is that the token booth clerk didn't know what that was about either. He probably didn't even know what I was talking about (nor did he care)! He probably figured that if he answered me in 'gibberish', I'd probably just go away, (which I did)!

MISS-----you BROKE my ROSE! (or) No More 'Flower Power'!

While this story did not actually take place on the subway, it occurred on the street on the WAY to the subway station, so I think it's appropriate to include it here rather than in the Impromptu section.

On my way home from the class I was teaching at a college in Manhattan, as I was nearing the subway station, there was a woman walking ahead of me who was holding a freshly cut rose in her hand, which she probably had just bought from a street vendor. As she was walking, she stopped suddenly and turned to chat with some man she obviously knew. It was a short conversation, maybe ten seconds or so, probably something like a "hello and good-bye". She then turned forward again to continue her journey, but just at that instant, another woman walking in the opposite direction accidently bumped into her, or, more accurately, they bumped into each other. The other woman kept on walking, but apparently the collision caused her rose to break off from the stem.

She then yelled out to the other woman, angrily, "MISS---you BROKE my ROSE"! The other woman turned around and mumbled some response, but I didn't hear what she said, then she continued on her way. I'm sure the readers won't think this story is really funny, but somehow, I get a kick out of it!

PART II. Buses, Charter Buses, City Buses, Multi-Day Bus Tours

WEEEEEEEEEEEEE! IT'S BETTER THAN CONEY ISLAND!

I was at the bus stop waiting for a bus one day. When the bus arrived, and a few passengers started to board, I heard the driver yell out "WEEEEEEEEEEEEEE, it's better than CONEY ISLAND! One woman passenger, already seated was giggling. I was wondering what that was all about. Than as the bus started moving I guess I found out. The shock absorbers or springs on the bus must have needed replacement, so the bus was rocking and rolling throughout the trip! Yes, Mr. Bus Driver, it WAS better than Coney Island! (Actually, at that time, ANYTHING was better than Coney Island! In the 50's and early 60's, Coney Island was a bustling amusement park, but after that it fell into kind of a state of disrepair, and although it still has some rides and attractions, it's not as great as it once was, and is certainly no match for the newer, more popular amusement parks. (Maybe someday it will return!).

THE COMEDIAN'S FAITHFUL FAN

I was on a small cruise ship and at every port we took a tour of the town and/or special or historical sites, usually in minivans or those yellow school buses (often called "cheese buses" due to their yellow cheese-like color). On these tours, either the bus driver narrates the tour directly, or there is a tour guide who does the narration. On one particular tour the bus driver acted as the narrator. This particular driver was a 'wanna-be' comedian, because, along with the narration, he added some jokes. That was fine with me, especially if the jokes were funny, but this guy's jokes were either not funny, minimally funny, or funny but so old that chances were you've heard them many times before. Anyway, he started out with an old joke about how a homeless man came up to him and said "sir, can you help me out? I haven't had a bite in a week!" The bus driver then said "so I bit him!" Funny??? A little bit, but I heard that joke when I was five years old, and probably hundreds of times since. Well, this woman sitting behind me probably never heard it before, and really must have thought it was funny, because she laughed loudly, encouraging the driver to tell more jokes because that one was so good! His next joke, a few minutes later also was old and not very funny: "a man in a restaurant calls the waiter over and tells him that the coffee tastes like mud, and the waiter tells him he should expect that because it was just ground this morning". Cute? Yes, a bit. Funny? Not really. Well, this same woman laughed at that one also, even harder than the first one! Another example: A man is in a restaurant eating chicken soup. He calls the waiter over and complains that he can't find any chicken in the chicken soup. The waiter replies "Don't expect to find any HORSE in the horse radish either! As expected, the woman BURST OUT laughing! To make a long story short, the tour lasted about two hours, and this went on and on for the full two hours. With every 'joke' the bus driver told (and NONE of them were really funny) she burst out laughing harder and harder---even more so that Ed McMahon on the Johnny Carson show! When I got off the bus at the end of the tour, some people stayed on the bus to go back into town to sightsee or shop, and she was one of them. As the bus pulled away, I could still hear her screaming "AH-HA-HA-HA-HA-HAAAAAAA!", even after the bus turned around the corner.

THE PAPAROZZI (or)
THE UNHAPPY NEIGHBOR

On a recent cruise to Europe, one of the ports of call was Liverpool, England, home of the Beatles. One of the tours offered was a visit to the Beatles' childhood homes, schools, clubs where they performed, etc. At their childhood homes, we got out of the bus to take pictures. The tour guide mentioned how nice the neighbors were, because they didn't complain about all the tour buses and all these people invading their privacy (of course, we know there are always exceptions)!

One stop was Paul McCartney's childhood home. The bus stopped around the corner and the tour guide and passengers got off to take pictures. Just then, I saw one of the neighbors, a woman seemingly quite annoyed, approach the bus driver. She complained that buses stay near her driveway all the time and block everyone. He told her that if she needed to exit her driveway he would gladly move. By that time the passengers finished taking their pictures and began to re-board the bus. The irate woman approached the tour director and you could see an argument was about to ensue! Most passengers just re-boarded the bus, but me, being the "yenter" (nosybody) that I am, stood around to 'enjoy' the argument! "Buses stop here NINE times a day!", she complained to the tour guide. The tour guide basically apologized, saying that people should understand that this is a 'famous' area. As the reprimand ensued, someone on the bus commented out loud "boy, if beauty is skin deep, she (the complaining neighbor) must have been born INSIDE-OUT!" Everyone laughed!

As the bus began to leave, many passengers waved goodbye to her, sarcastically. I also waved, but felt like laughing, pointing my finger at her, being my obnoxious self, and saying "ah-ha-ha-ha-ha-haaaaaaaaaaaaaa!

All these tourists and buses annoy you all day. Too bad! Ah-ha-ha-ha-ha-haaaaaaaaaaa!".

THE HAND IS QUICKER THAN THE EYE!
(or) Passing the Bar Exam

I was visiting Seattle and found out that there were tours operated by private bus companies to Mount Rainier. Being an amateur geologist and a "volcano freak", I wasted no time booking a tour!

The first problem was that on the way up, the bus broke down, and the driver called the office and was told to drop us off at a nearby motel, and a replacement bus would be there in about an hour. Well, it took about 3 hours for the new bus to arrive. We (the passengers) were all pissed, but the new driver said he would spend extra time at the Mount Rainier area to make up for the time we lost.

Anyway, on the way back the driver stopped the bus and told us turn around in our seats and face the back of the bus. There was a big window at the rear of the bus and he said if we look out of it we could see the entire Mount Rainier from behind. Everybody turned around in their seats to have a look, and it really was an impressive sight—seeing the mountain in all its splendor from behind, especially the snow-covered top! Anyway, as I was turning to see the view, this woman in the seat in front of me was also turning, and suddenly she looks me in the face and shouts "OW-OW-OW-OW-STOP-STOP-STOP-STOP!!!! I was amazed! I couldn't figure out what she was talking about! "What is this woman screaming about? I thought to myself! Then I realized what happened. Behind all the seats there was a long cylindrical metal bar. I guess it was put there as a safety gadget to hold on to if the bus was turning or going up- or downhill. Well, if you hold onto that bar and push it, it will push onto the back of the seat in front of it. If someone has their hands on the bar, and the passenger behind it pushes it, their hands will get 'pressed' between the bar and back of the seat---somewhat of a painful experience, depending on how much force is being pressed! So what really happened was that when we all turned around in our seats to see the mountain from behind, that woman put her hands around the bar, and I pushed on it at the same time, unknowingly! So when she screamed "OW-OW-OW-OW-STOP-STOP-STOP-STOP!!!", and I finally realized what the problem was, I let go of the bar! She didn't really get hurt, but I guess having your hands pressed against a bar and back of the seat like that is no fun! Anyway, I, being my ole' obnoxious self, teased her about it all the way back!

THE BIGGER THEY COME, THE HARDER THEY FALL! (or) "Heeeeeeey, Do the Mouse Yeah!"

I was riding on a bus in Brooklyn in the rear section, where I like to sit so I can stretch out a bit. Some big, tall "tough guy" gets on shortly thereafter and he begins to mumble things at other passengers, to let us know that he's big and tough! This continues for a few more stops, with everyone just ignoring him, or at least pretending to ignore him. You could see that this guy thought he was a real 'hot-shot'; that nobody would dare answer him back because we were all afraid of him.

All of a sudden, 'Superman' gets on the bus, a guy even taller and more macho than him! He sees what's going on and confronts the other guy: "you think you're a TOUGH guy? How'd you like to take ME on!" The first guy now becomes a little mouse! "Oh no, Oh no, I was just kidding around" he says. You could sense the fear in his voice. Superman now continues to challenge the guy, but the guy kept backing off, becoming more and more of a mouse! Superman continued to challenge this guy, inviting him to "step off the bus", but the mouse kept apologizing and claiming he was just kidding around before with the other passengers. This went on for about another fifteen minutes, until finally, Superman got off the bus at his stop, sneering at the mouse as he exited.

Wouldn't you know, as soon as Superman got off the bus, the mouse became a tough guy again! ---mumbling things to the other passengers (who continued to ignore him). When I finally reached my stop, I felt like saying to him "you'd better shut up or I'll call Superman back!" (But, I guess, being a mouse myself, I just kept quiet and got off)!

THE CARNIVAL OF VENICE (or) Just Whistle While You Ride (The Bus)!(or) FINALLY, My Chance to Conduct the Band!

I have taken many vacation bus tours over the years, some lasting a few days, others lasting a couple of weeks. On these trips you meet many fellow travelers, but most of the time, once the tour is over, you never hear from them again, and often you completely forget them! Anyway, on one particular trip I ran into a married couple that remembered me from a previous bus tour, and I shook their hands and said that I remembered them also. Truthfully, this was a complete lie, as I didn't remember them at all! Anyway, the husband was almost always whistling a tune while the bus was traveling, and it was always the SAME song, The Carnival of Venice! Can you imagine riding on a bus day after day and hearing the SAME song being whistled by the SAME guy over and over again? Well, one day while he was whistling his tune, I turned to the guy sitting next to me and started swinging my arms and hands as if I were a band leader conducting an orchestra while they played The Carnival of Venice. I thought the guy would immediately understand this and would laugh, but apparently he didn't. So I did this a few more times, and the guy just stared at me. Finally he asked "are YOU on DRUGS????" I had to explain it to him: "don't you hear The Carnival of Venice?"

Then he smiled. But to this day I still wonder if he understood what I was doing. The 'Carnival of Venice' guy continued to whistle it throughout the rest of the trip! I wonder if he's still whistling it right now! (And he ain't just whistlin' DIXIE!)

SPLISH-PLASH I WAS TAKING A BATH!
(or) The Oil Man's Dream: IT'S A GUSHER!

It was a hot summer day. I was on a bus in Queens, sitting all the way in the back near the window; these are my favorite seats on a bus! I was sitting by the right rear window, which is on the door side of the bus. Opposite me, sitting by the left rear window, (driver's side) was a guy, about 20 years old, holding a still unopened can of soda. I thought nothing of that, since it was a very hot day, and what better way to cool off than having a nice cold can of soda! I was wondering, though, WHEN was he going to open it?

As I was looking out the window, all of a sudden I hear "PSSSSSSSST"! Yes, he finally opened the can of soda! I don't know if he had inadvertently shaken the can before opening or if the soda become too warm, but I glanced over to see what that noise was, only to see that it had SQUIRTED all over him---face, neck, and shirt! I immediately pulled a 'Sergeant Schultz'---turning my face back toward the window, whistling to myself silently, making believe that nothing had happened ("I saw nothing, NO-THING!"). After he got off the bus a few stops later, I began to laugh HYSTERICALLY, 'CRACKING UP'! What an IDIOT that guy was! ---Didn't he KNOW you don't open a can of warm soda, or a can of soda that was shaken up?

What was even more interesting was that when I told this story to my high school students a few months later, they asked me why I waited until the guy got off the bus before I laughed. I told them the obvious: that had I laughed while he was still on the bus he would have gotten mad and probably would have HIT me! Their response to that was "So WHAT? ---

YOU have FISTS!" Even more interesting was that the students who said this were girls!

"SNAP"!

I was on a bus tour run by a nature-sightseeing company. They took us on all sorts of visits to geological and wildlife areas and at night we stayed at various hotels and motels. One particular trip took us to Yellowstone and Glacier National Parks. Most of the meals, if not all, were included in the itinerary and we ate our meals together, family style, usually at one large table. There were usually 12 to 15 participants on each tour.

One evening we stopped for dinner in a restaurant and we all sat together at a large, long table with wooden chairs. There were many smaller tables in the room for families and other tour groups, etc. The backs of the wooden chairs were not solid but rather made of long wooden pegs arranged in a vertical fashion, like the spickets of a wooden fence (to make a good analogy). Most of the group was already seated when I decided to sit down, and other people were seated at the other tables in the room. All of a sudden, as I sat down (the room had been quiet and serene) there was an eardrum-shattering "SNAP"! It was so loud that many of the people in the restaurant SCREAMED "OHHHHHH"! "What was THAT?", they wondered. Not being exactly a lightweight, I guess I sat down in the chair a little to quickly and with a little too much force, so one of those wooden pegs SNAPPED in half! It sounded almost like a gunshot! That's what you can call sitting down with a "BANG"!

RING THE BELL AND RUN AWAY! (or) Oops!.... Wrong Number!

I was a typical kid when I was nine or ten, always getting into trouble, especially when I hung around some of my neighborhood friends (I might have been a 'typical' kid, but I'm certainly not a 'typical' adult!). One 'game' we often played was "ring the bell and run away". We rang someone's door bell, and quickly ran away, so that they would open their door for nothing! To us, in our warped minds, it was 'fun'! We rarely, if ever, got into trouble for it, since we were far gone by the time the person opened his or her door!

On a recent trip to the Catskills, we went with a 'group' who chartered a bus. The bus picked up passengers in different boroughs, so we had to meet the bus in specific locations at specific times. When we arrived at the location, in front of a large apartment house, the bus hadn't yet arrived. The weather was a bit chilly (it was about 7 AM), so we decided to wait in the lobby of the apartment house, where we saw some chairs. The problem was that there was a double-door entrance to the lobby, and in order to get inside we would have to be 'buzzed' in by ringing someone's bell. One of the women in the group said she knew whose bell to ring, because that party was involved in arranging the bus pick-ups, but she wasn't sure of the exact spelling of his name, so she wasn't sure which bell to ring, since some names have similar spellings. So she rang the bell once, but there was no 'buzz', so she rang it a second time... no buzz, so she rang it a third, then a fourth, then a fifth time...no buzz, so she rang it a sixth, then a seventh time, ...etc. Finally, the tenant whose bell she had been ringing came out YELLING, SCREAMING, in his pajamas "Do you know Vat TIME it tis?" he screamed, in a foreign accent. Obviously, we woke him up! He was not happy about it! "Sorry", she explained…...." I guess I must have been wringing the wrong bell". He walked back to his apartment, still yelling, screaming, cursing, using every four-letter word he knew (and he knew quite many!). Obviously, this tenant was no quite so 'forgiving' (but at least we had some chairs to sit on as we waited for the bus in a nice warm lobby!). He walk back to his apartment.

POOR BILL!

I was on an overnight bus trip a few years ago. On the bus, besides other passengers, were a man, (I'll call him 'Bill' in order not to use his *real* name) probably in his early 50's, his wife, their child (a boy about 5 years old) and his mother-in-law. The guy didn't appear to be too affluent, which was probably why they were traveling by bus. Anyway, on a long bus trip, sometimes passengers get up and stand for a while, to break the monotony of sitting all those hours. The four were all seated across from each other. Anyway, after finishing up a rest stop, Bill was standing in the aisle, next to his wife, child, and mother-in-law who were seated, and they were engaged in a conversation. Suddenly, Bill's wife made a motion of discomfort, kind of pushed Bill away a few inches, and said "OH BILL—you're LEANING against me, as if she were annoyed, making a facial expression of pain! A few minutes later, Bill sat down next to her, and she again made an expression of 'discomfort', and said "OH BILL, you're CRUSHING me"! A few minutes later, as they were still engaged in conversation between Bill's wife and her mother, and Bill was standing between them, Bill's wife again kind of pushed him a few inches to the side, and cried out "OH BILL, you're BLOCKING my view!"

A few minutes later, as Bill was standing between them and counting the money he had left in his wallet (which, from the expression on his face, was running out!), Bill's wife cried out "OH BILL! Can't you stand still? You're making me DIZZY!" Eventually, Bill's mother-in-law asked him a few questions, just for the sake of helping him get his mind off being henpecked by her daughter. I could see she felt sorry for him! For the next ten minutes, until the bus started moving again and everyone sat down, all I kept hearing every few minutes was "OH BILL (THIS)" and "OH BILL (THAT)"! All I kept thinking to myself was **"POOR BILL"!**

ON THE *ROAD* IT'S OK, BUT *HERE* IT'S NOT OK???

I was on a nature tour of the Pacific Northwest one summer-- Washington, Oregon-- with a tour company that specialized in nature studies—biology, geology, flora and fauna, etc. We traveled through all sorts of environments, identifying and studying the various plants and animals. We saw animals such as black bears, grizzlies, elk, moose, marmots, beavers, raccoons, ---you name it, we probably saw it! We traveled in a minibus—not as large as a regular tour bus, but much larger than a van. The group consisted of men and women of a variety of ages and sizes, as well as a few teens and a couple of octogenarians!

Anyway, one day as we were riding on the road, the tour guide suddenly asked the bus driver to pull off to the side of the road and stop, and then he got out of the bus. Nobody on the bus knew why he exited, nor where he was going, so we all looked at each other and started coming up with all kinds of hypotheses. Suddenly, he returned with the carcass of a dead animal—road kill—I think it was a raccoon or a beaver. The idea was to show us an example of the animals that live in the area, and what better way to do this than to show us the local road kill! Women on the bus started SCREAMING---"GET THAT THING OUT OF HERE------GET THAT THING OUT OF HERE!!!", so he brought it back outside and tossed it into the grass. When he returned many of the women told him to PLEASE never do that again! "On the *ROAD* it's OK, but *HERE* it's *NOT* "OK???' he answered. I just sat back and laughed!

IT SHOULD HAPPEN TO YOU! (or)
The Wild Barfer!

I spent a few days vacationing one summer at a hotel in the Catskills—upstate New York. I don't even recall the name of the hotel—I think it was called "The Majestic", but it doesn't matter anyway because like most Catskill hotels, it's probably out of business by now! Anyway, I think it was a 'single's' weekend—probably Labor Day weekend, and, as part of the package, we were brought there from Manhattan and back by a charter bus. There were probably about 50 seats on the bus, most of which were filled. Most people who sat together (one at the window seat, the other at the aisle seat) didn't really know each other, except perhaps if they had met previously during the (short) vacation.

Anyway, after the hotel stay, the bus took off shortly after lunch, and most people engorged themselves in the dining room that day, to be sure they got their 'money's worth'---I think you know what I mean! Maybe it was because the bus driver was going a bit too fast, or maybe/also because they engorged themselves, one by one people started throwing up! Actually, it was probably only three or four, but it sure SEEMED like everybody! Near the front of the bus two people were seated together, a man in his 60's dressed in a suit, and a younger guy—probably in his mid-twenties. For most of the trip, they seemed to be talking and getting along nicely, until I heard, again, "BARF......BARF.... BARRRRRRRF"! Apparently, the younger guy had to throw up very fast, and BARFED on the floor just below his seat! Apparently, some of the barf SPLATTERED on the other guy's pants! Well, needless to say, the 'friendship' was soon over! The older guy began cursing at the barfer at the top of his lungs! The barfer repeated several times "I'm SORRY......I'm SORRY......I'm

SORRY!" But the other guy (the guy whose pants got barfed on/the "barfee") continued to curse him out! Finally, the barfer, quite frustrated, screamed out "MISTER----I said I'm SORRY---now SHUT UP!" A woman sitting behind them said to the 'barfee': "why don't you quiet down? He SAID he was SORRY!" "It should happen to YOU!", replied the 'barfee'.

HELP! I'VE LOCKED MYSELF IN THE BATHROOM----AND I CAN'T GET OUT!

I was on a bus from the Catskills to Manhattan, and the ride takes about 2 and a half hours. There is a small bathroom in the back of the bus—it's about the size of a clothes closet! On the trip an elderly woman used the facility and about one half hour later, she started BANGING on the door, and we heard "HELP! HELP! I'M LOCKED IN, and I CAN'T get out"! Sound familiar? I and several other passengers tried to open the door, but because of the WAY she locked it from inside, it was impossible to get open! Finally, the driver pulled over to the side of the road and tried, but even HE couldn't open the bathroom door!

Don't ask me exactly HOW, but somehow he climbed partly through the back window of the bus and after about 15 minutes, he managed to get partly inside the bathroom and 'free' her. Half of his body was outside the rear window, and the other half was still inside the bus!

ENCORE! ENCORE! (or) **Tubby the Tuba!**

When I began junior high school at age 12, my class had a daily period of instrumental music. On the first day of music class, we were allowed to choose whatever instrument we wanted to learn how to play, which would be "our" instrument for the entire year. Materialistic as I was, I chose the biggest, loudest instrument I could find, which happened to be the tuba! You should have SEEN this thing---it looked like it had been through both world wars! It was dented and scratched up beyond belief! It was old, tarnished, dirty, and quite decrepit! The music teacher allowed, actually encouraged us to take our instruments home each weekend, in order to practice on them. I took the tuba home almost every weekend. I wanted to show the WORLD that I could PLAY that MONSTROSITY! I lived about a mile away from the school, and usually took the city bus to school and back, especially if I were carrying that MONSTROSITY with me!

To make a long story short, no sooner did I sit down on the bus, I began to play songs!

The only thing worse than the appearance of that tuba was the way I SOUNDED on it! I played songs of which I did not know the notes, nor what valves to push to play the notes even if I knew them! I once even went on a kiddie TV show called "Wonderama" to play that monstrosity!

I guess the passengers were amused by the concert, either THAT or they felt sorry for me (maybe a combination of BOTH!), because the next thing I knew, PENNIES came flying at me! Then NICKELS! When I emptied the tuba by turning it upside-down when I got home, I even found some QUARTERS! (Remember, those were the mid-60's, when quarters were more like DOLLARS)! Whoever said that New Yorkers weren't generous didn't witness this great event!

DON'T TREAD ON ME! (or) "Put Your Shoe on my Shoooooooouuullllllllder......"

I was on a Greyhound bus trip, and on these trips, there are usually many stops made, with people getting on and off. Sometimes they're not too crowded, and people can spread out across two seats, while other times they are crowded and every seat is occupied. It usually depends on the route traveled, time of day, time of year, day of the week, and many other factors.

Anyway, on this one trip, it was semi-crowded. Some people had an empty seat next to them so they could spread out, and some did not. One guy had an empty seat next to him, so he decided to spread out by lying down across them. Across from him, in the opposite aisle, there were two people, one occupying each seat. I was sitting in the rear section of the bus, so I could see things that were going on up front. This guy who was lying down, probably without realizing it, constantly jerked his feet, and he had his shoes on, so every time he jerked his foot forward, his shoe touched the guy's arm in the opposite aisle, so that his shoe put a dust patch on the other guy's jacket. The first time this happened, the guy looked at his jacket and just brushed off the dust with his hand. He didn't try to wake the other guy up and ask him, nicely, to be careful because his shoe was putting dust on his jacket. He just brushed the dust off, probably thinking this was just a fluke. A few minutes later, the same thing happened, and, again, they guy just brushed the dust off his jacket without saying anything to the other guy. A few minutes later, the same thing happened, with the same action by the other guy (just brushing off the dust).

To make a long story short, this went on and on, ---the guy's shoe dirtying the other guy's jacket, and the other guy just brushing the dust off!

I sat in my seat in the back of the bus and watched and watched and laughed and laughed! Why he never said "BOO" to the other guy was beyond me! Maybe what he should've done was to take off his own shoe and smack the other guy in the head a few times!

COWBOYS AND AIR CONDITIONERS

I was on a cross country bus tour from New York to the Canadian Rockies, and we stayed overnight at a motel near Madison, Wisconsin. It was hot all day, so when I entered my room the first thing I did was to turn on the air conditioner. The next thing I did was to turn on the TV. I flipped through the channels with the remote, but nothing worthwhile was playing. I settled for a cowboy movie, even though cowboy movies are not my cup of tea. A scene came on where they were shooting with pistols, which is certainly not unusual for a cowboy movie. But something was "different" about this scene. The gunshots seemed awfully loud! I thought to myself "gee, these guns sound very loud, it's almost as if the shots are being fired right here in my room!" Suddenly I saw smoke (but NOT on the TV)! "What the hell?", I thought to myself, "what is this, some kind of new technology where the gun smoke comes out of the picture tube?" Then I realized what actually happened. The air conditioner was malfunctioning! The 'gunshots' and smoke were coming out of the air conditioner, not from the movie! I went to the front desk and had my room changed! Talk about serendipity--- 'gunshots' and smoke from the air conditioner during a cowboy movie!

THE CASE OF THE "CASOKLEPTOMANIAC"

What actually IS a "casokleptomaniac"? Well, actually, there IS no such word in the English language—I made it up myself! So what is it supposed to mean? Well, a kleptomaniac is a person who steals things—not necessarily because he needs them, but just because they are "there"! A *caso*kleptomaniac, then, would be a kleptomaniac who steals suitcases and luggage.

Such an event occurred a number of years ago when I was on a vacation bus tour, I don't remember exactly where, might have been in Ontario, or Nova Scotia, New Brunswick—somewhere in that northern region.

Anyway, on those tours we stayed overnight at various hotels and motels, and the next morning, an hour or two before we re-boarded the bus to continue the trip, we were told to put our luggage outside our rooms so that the staff and bus driver and tour guide can re-load them onto the bus. This particular motel contained several buildings at ground level, so when we put our luggage outside for re-loading, we were actually putting it OUTSIDE—in front of our doors. Anyway, one morning when we were re-boarding the bus and the luggage was being re-loaded, the guy that sat next to me noticed that he did not see one of his suitcases in the pile. He thought, at first, that they might have already re-loaded it with some others, so he didn't inquire about it. But, just to be sure, before we took off, he asked the tour guide and bus driver to check and see. As you've probably, guessed, his suitcase was missing—STOLEN! He told the driver and tour guide that earlier, he saw a guy walking around the motel grounds, and that he looked "suspicious"! They then reported it to motel manager who called the police. When he described the guy he saw, the police said they thought they knew whom it might be, because there was a guy in that area who had been arrested for that before. They said they would hunt him down and see if they could find his suitcase or get the culprit to confess. The bus had to continue on its journey, and I don't know if he ever got his suitcase back. The guy sat next to me as we traveled and we spoke for a while about the theft, and I was very supportive and empathetic, at least *superficially*. While this incident certainly wasn't 'funny', I couldn't help get the THOUGHT out of my obnoxious head of pointing and saying to him: "HA!-HA! They stole your suitcase!".

Look Out BELOOOOOOOOOOOOOW!

I took a one-day bus tour to Howe Caverns in upstate New York. I had been there several times in the past, but, having a background in geology, I like to re-visit now and then to see the cave features such as the stalactites and stalagmites. To enter the caverns, you must first take an elevator down a few hundred feet. The caverns are relatively dark, even though there are electric lights. As we (about 40 people on the bus tour) started to walk into the caverns, there was a woman on crutches with us. She was lagging behind the group and walking slowly and cautiously. I thought to myself that this woman should not be walking alone, in dim light, especially with crutches, since she might fall, especially since part of the path is on an incline, downward, and it could be slippery. Within a few seconds, we heard "CRASH—BOOM"! She fell, as I had feared would happen, and everyone came running. Luckily, she wasn't hurt, or at least that's what she said. The tour director then advised her to stay behind until the rest of the passengers returned at the end of the tour. I later found out that this woman came on the tour with her niece, a teenager who ran to the front of the tour line and left her in the dust. While this story about someone falling is not 'funny', the whole idea of someone trying to walk through dark caverns with crutches wasn't the smartest thing to do! One need not be a rocket scientist to figure that out!

Hey Kid----GET OUT-A- HERE! ----Ya BOTHER Me!

I was on a multi day bus tour which went to northern Ontario and nearby regions, including an old gold mine and an area near a river that contained many fossils. Most of the passengers were elderly or recently retired, but there was a middle aged couple as well, with their son, probably about 10 or 11 years old. That kind was quite a character and quite a handful! He was kind of like a clone of Dennis The Menace, if you can picture it! Within a few hours after the trip began, everyone on the bus knew this kid's name, whereas most passengers never knew anyone else's name even after more than a week of traveling together! Someone remarked that he was the kind of kid that you would tell to go outside and play in the traffic!

Anyway, one day when the bus stopped for a 'break', or what we call a "rest stop", the kid walked around and caught a large frog which was hopping around in the grass (there was a lake or pond nearby). He was showing the frog to a few people who were walking around, browsing. When I saw the frog, I said to him "Hey kid, when the bus gets ready to leave, why don't you bring that frog onto the bus and show all the old ladies what a beautiful frog you found! He smiled and thanked me for the idea! Unfortunately, by the time the bus was ready to leave, the frog got away. What a shame! I'm sure all those old ladies would have loved to see that beautiful frog!

UUUUUUUH. ERRRRRRRR. EGGGGGGGGG. AGGGGGGGGG. EHHHHHHH. IRRRRGGGGGGHHH. (or) "Variations in the language of "uuuhhh"!

I remember one day, in math class in junior high school/8th grade, the teacher said" somebody in this class is making weird sounds, and God help that person if I find out who it is"! She was looking at me when she said that, and for good reason-----it was ME who was making those sounds! You probably wonder WHY I was making those sounds. I wasn't doing it to be disruptive. Actually I didn't even realize that I was making the sounds! What happened was that a few days before, on TV, some foreign politician, I believe he was from a European country, was being interviewed. We all know how many people constantly say "uuuhhh" or "uuummm" when they are speaking, some more than others! Well, foreigners do the same thing, but they do it with different accents. So when I saw that politician on TV using all those "uuuhhhs" (in his accent), it stuck in my mind!

So for whatever reason, that day in math class, I suddenly remembered that guy on TV, and I was imitating him, in my mind, not realizing that others in class or the teacher had heard it!

So, you may ask, what the hell does that have to do with cruises? OK, let me tell you. A few years ago I went on a cruise to Europe, going to places such as Iceland, Greenland, England, Holland, and a few other places. At each port, there were bus tours (shore excursions) available, and I went on many of them. On each tour, a tour guide usually accompanies the driver, and he is equipped with a microphone and speakers. Most of them also use "uuuhhh's" when they speak, but their "uuuhhhs" are not the same "uuuhhhs" that we usually hear--- they are heard in THEIR accents.

You probably would not believe the strange versions of "uuuhhh" in different countries. It's really amazing---how even the "uuuhhh" lingo varies with latitude and longitude! All I can suggest is that the next time you go to a foreign country and go on a bus tour with a tour guide, keep your ears open—sensitize them---to the sounds of the "uuuhhh" lingo of the region!

THE TREE THAT WAS NOT THERE! (or)
The Incredible Shrinking Bush (or)
The Tree or NOT the Tree!

When I was an undergraduate in college, I took a summer course called "Field Studies in Botany". In that course, we traveled to different ecological sites to identify and study the species of plants, shrubs, and trees present. The college chartered buses to takes us to these sites and bring us back home to the campus. The trips usually began early in the morning and often ended late at night. We went to various fields, forests, swampy areas, beaches and sandy areas, mountainous areas, salt marshes, lakes, ponds, etc. There were about 20 students in the class, as well as a botany professor who was an orchid specialist.

Anyway, another science professor had a teenage son who was interested in botany and the natural sciences, so she asked the botany professor if her son could come along on some of the trips, and he was happy to allow it, after all, she was a colleague of his.

During these trips I kind of befriended the teenager, and as we hiked we discussed many things, usually science topics. Although I was officially a biology major, I was sort of a philosophy minor, having taken numerous philosophy courses such as introductory philosophy, history of philosophy, Oriental philosophy, metaphysics, and others. I introduced him to the philosophy of Renee Descartes, the philosopher who questioned 'reality', wondering if anything was 'real', usually stating that objects that we see are really not there, that these objects are just in our mind—that they are figments of our imaginations, and our own existence was questionable! He coined the phrase *"Cogito Ergo Sum" (I THINK, therefore I EXIST),* when trying to answer the question of whether a person really exists. In other words, the mere fact that a person can think and has consciousness proves that he really exists, that he is 'real'. However, physical objects that we see and touch may or may NOT be real, since they are not conscious nor do they 'think', at least insofar as we know! Anyway, after discussing this with him for hours and days at end, he began to get tired of it and actually started getting annoyed with it, and with ME! He kept telling me to stop talking about "that STUPID philosophy", and he even told the botany professor that I believe in mind over matter and that I was claiming that nothing was real—that everything was fake---just an illusion! The botany professor listened and said to me "well, when you get your GRADE, don't worry, IT'S REAL"!

Anyway, to try to make a long story short, I kept teasing the kid, constantly telling him that nothing was 'real', that everything was fake, and he kept getting more and more annoyed! He kept telling me to "SHUT-UP with that STUPID PHILOSOPHY"! and after a while he stayed away from me, because of my obnoxiousness, which I enjoyed!

Anyway, these trips involved long hikes which were very strenuous, sometimes we hiked for several miles, people, including me, often walked slower and lagged behind, and sometimes the professor had to send out fellow students as 'search parties' to locate those that were 'lost' or lagging behind! One day, this kid lagged behind, and we didn't know what happened to him---was he lagging behind or did he get lost? A few search parties went out to find him but were unsuccessful. Finally, he showed up, all tired and out of breath, bitching and complaining about the hike, frustrated that he couldn't keep up, and he yelled about the tough time he had to find the group, and he mentioned that he was so frustrated and so pissed off that he accidently ripped a Rhododendron (a shrub that makes flowers) out of the ground when he grabbed it to hold as a support when was climbing up a hill! In my obnoxiousness, I had the urge to start teasing him again, but I was afraid that he might actually hit me in that pissed-off state so I said nothing.

When the trip ended and the bus lets us off by the college campus that evening, and he had calmed down at bit, I walked over to him and said that I was sorry for the bad experience he had, and he thanked me. Then I said to him, whispering, "by the way---don't feel so bad about the Rhododendron that you ripped out of the ground". He asked me why, and I said, again in a whisper, "because it wasn't really there ANYWAY"! As I noticed that he was getting red in the face, I ran away!

I don't know what college he eventually went to, nor what he majored in, but I'm SURE it WASN'T PHILOSOPHY!

PART III. Experiences on AMTRAK and Multi-Day Rail Travel

"CHOO-CHOO CHEWIES"

I was on AMTRAK in the dining car, seated with three other people, none of whom knew each other. Being a vegetarian, I often have difficulty ordering from a menu, but, to their credit, AMTRAK is smart enough to have at least one vegetarian dish at every meal. However, AMTRAK is almost always "out" of something (at least that's been MY experience), and, in this case, they were "out" of the vegetarian meal.

Now I had a problem. There were no other vegetarian meals to order. I looked through the entire menu and managed to find a substitute; it was called "CHOO-CHOO CHEWIES" and was actually cheese-filled ravioli. The problem was that it was listed only in the "children's" menu! Luckily, and to his credit, the waiter understood my problem and agreed to serve it. When it arrived, it came in a small cardboard box, with colorful cartoon characters drawn all over the outside (probably like Mickey Mouse, Donald Duck, Daffy Duck, Porky Pig, Superman, Flip The Frog, Big Bird, Smurf, etc.)! You should have seen the LOOKS I was getting from the other passengers as they ate their steaks, roast beef, and turkey dinners, and I ate my "Choo-Choo-Chewies"!

A SPIT IN TIME (But please, not on MINE!)

The dining car on AMTRAK has only a limited number of tables and seats, so people who don't know each other are usually seated together. It's a good way to meet people and have a conversation with fellow passengers, although lasting friendships will rarely result. Anyway, I was seated with a man and his young daughter, probably about 8 years old. We conversed throughout the meal (I don't remember about what). At one point, as the father was talking to me, a tiny piece of food shot out of his mouth onto his daughter's plate, although I don't think he realized it—but SHE did! She yelled out "DAAAAAAD!, you SPIT on my PLATE!!!….. dis-GUST-ing!!!". I still crack up to this day whenever I think about it!

THE 'TOMATO SEED EXPRESS'

On another occasion in the AMTRAK dining car, I was seated with a woman and her elderly but vibrant mother. The dinner meal usually starts with a small garden salad, and AMTRAK has a habit of adding a few cherry tomatoes into it. That's a good idea, but the problem is that they add WHOLE cherry tomatoes, rather than cutting them in half.

All of a sudden, I thought I saw something shoot across the side of my face. Then the elderly woman asked "did I squirt anybody"? She explained that after placing the cherry tomato into her mouth, she bit down and it 'SQUIRTED'! I looked around at my clothes but saw nothing, so I told her not to worry, it probably went onto the floor. Later on, before leaving the table, I noticed the man at the table behind me, and there were tomato seeds all over the back of his sport jacket! Lesson to be learned: when making salads, NEVER add WHOLE cherry tomatoes---cut then into halves first! (Actually, the scenario could have been worse----the tomato could have squired into somebody's face, eyes, or mouth!).

BIGFOOT!

Do you believe in Bigfoot? Sasquatch? The Abominable Snowman? Yeti? These are all synonyms for the same 'beings'. I wouldn't say I definitely believe, but I wouldn't say I definitely don't believe. What does that have to do with this book, anyway? Or about AMTRAK? OK, let me tell you.

In the AMTRAK dining car, people are seated at the same table randomly. This is done to save space, and it gives you a chance to meet people and socialize. Anyway, at my table I met an elderly couple from New Mexico. We began to speak about Roswell and UFO's, and the husband stated that he really believed aliens crashed there! I told him I was undecided about that but that I had an open mind (and one that is a bit warped!). Next, he asked me if I believe in Bigfoot. Again, I told him I was undecided but had an open mind. Then he told me that he definitely believed in Bigfoot because he SAW one! He said he and his wife were driving in Oregon on a road near a heavily forested area. It was about 8 AM with few cars on the road. It had recently rained and there was a waterfall nearby and a few small stores. Suddenly, BIGFOOT crosses the road a short distance in front of them! He was over seven feet tall, stocky, and very hairy! He didn't even look at the road for cars! It happened so fast neither he nor his wife (who corroborated the story) realized what they saw for a few seconds! They were startled! The husband said that he had hunted all his life and knows that what they saw was not a bear, nor a deer, elk, and it walked on two legs.

I told them that they should have stopped the car, gotten out, and yelled "HEY BIGFOOT! ---HOW YA' DOING"!

PART IV. Experiences on Cruise Ships, Boats, Freighter Cruises, Riverboat Cruises

A SCENE FROM THE THREE STOOGES (I) (or) An Object in Motion Remains in Motion...... Unless There's a Collision!

I was on a cruise ship, to where I don't quite remember. A was walking along the inside hallway at a relatively rapid pace. A waiter was also walking in the connecting hallway, carrying a large metal tray above his head—you know, how they hold it up high with one hand. He was walking at a fast pace. On his tray were empty champagne or wine glasses. Apparently, he was in a rush to get them to the kitchen to be washed. He must have been carrying them away from some kind of reception where alcohol was served. So we were both walking at fairly rapid paces in perpendicular directions, and we did not, nor could we, see each other. Anyway, as I was walking, I spotted him walking with his tray of empty glasses perpendicular towards me, and I'm sure he also spotted me. We saw each other walking rapidly and figured there would be no problem, because if both of us kept up at our current speeds, everything would be fine. For whatever reason, after I first saw him, I stopped short----I don't know why---maybe I was curious to see what he was carrying on the tray. To make a long story short, because I stopped short, he couldn't quite stop in time, and we kind-of COLLIDED ("CRASH-BOOM")! There were wine and champagne glasses all over the floor! Luckily, I don't think any of them actually broke and neither of us was hurt, but he sure uttered a lot of 'explicatives' at me, asking why I stopped short. I said "sorry" and went on my way, laughing obnoxiously as usual, realizing that this might be part of a book someday (like NOW!)

A SCENE FROM THE THREE STOOGES II

I was on a small cruise ship cruising along the Mississippi River—a real nice, quiet, serene vacation! I was in the dining room at dinner with several other passengers, two of whom were also Ph.D.'s but with whom I was not familiar at all. (that made three of us, myself included; the "Ph.D. Table"!

The dinner attire was formal, as a jacket and tie were required... At a nearby table, a waiter was carrying a large metal tray with plates of food. In a scene directly out of the Three Stooges, he DROPS a plate of food right on top of a passenger's sport jacket! Of, course, he apologized exuberantly, and the maitre D' and other waiters immediately brought him a replacement jacket and sent his soiled jacket out for cleaning.

I, in my obnoxiousness, began laughing uncontrollably, but I tried my best to hide it! I tried to camouflage the laughing as much as possible, putting my hand over my mouth to hide it, biting my lip, looking downward, covering my face, but these were to no avail! I was laughing so hard and trying to hide it that at times I almost CHOKED! What was funny was NOT that the guy's jacket got messed up, but rather the WAY it happened—suddenly, instantly, without warning…. "SPLASH"! All that was needed at that point was to heat Curly yelling "Woooo-Wooooo-Wooooo-Woooo-Wooooo-Woooooo-Wooooo-Wooooo"!

What really bothered me, though, was WHAT those other two Ph.D.'s at my table probably thought of me as a fellow Ph.D.! They probably couldn't figure out what I was laughing about through the entire meal! If the KNEW what I was laughing about, they probably thought it wasn't so funny or funny at all, and probably thought that I was CRAZY (which I AM!). They SAID nothing to me, and they didn't even LOOK at me, or at least tried not to! They probably started to wonder what kind of university would grant their highest degree to a guy like ME!

"ToooooooooooooooooooooT"!

I was a passenger one summer on a small freight ship that traveled from Newfoundland up the coast of Labrador and back—the trip lasted about two weeks. Very interesting and educational! Most pf the Labrador inhabitants live in small villages along the coast. The main industries are fishing and crabbing. The soil is rocky and there is little topsoil, so agriculture is lacking, and most fruits and vegetables must be imported.

A few days before starting the cruise, I attended a concert at Seaside Park in the Coney Island section of Brooklyn. These were so popular in the local neighborhoods that seating was always filled up, and people could bring their own chairs, pillows, blankets, etc. I usually chose to sit on the grass, and I sat in a yoga position for several hours, getting up only occasionally to stretch my legs. Anyway, I must have done some damage to my knees from sitting in that position all those hours, because for a couple of weeks afterward, I had severe, arthritic-like knee pain, something I very rarely get, and walking was painful! Anyway, as my freighter cruise was to begin in a couple of days, you can guess that the knee pain followed me on the cruise!

To make a long story short, when we visited one of the ports on the Labrador coast, we were told by the cruise staff that we would there for about two hours, so that gave me time to walk around and explore, even WITH my knee pain! I rarely wear watches, so I had to estimate the time remaining or ask someone else what the correct time was. The ship usually blew its horn when it was getting ready to depart. As I was ready to head back to the ship (I estimated I still had at least 30 minutes left), I noticed a very strange outcrop (rock formation) further up the road. As an amateur geologist, I just HAD to walk over and explore it (even with my knee pain and slow pace)! It really was a beautiful rock formation and it seemed to just "POP UP" out of nowhere. I took many pictures of it and walked on it and around it. I knew this was using up time, but my estimate was that I still had enough time to examine it and get back to the ship---I figured I still had at least 15 minutes.

All of a sudden, I heard "TooooooooooooooooooooT"—obviously, this meant that the ship was ready to sail out. I couldn't imagine how it was ready to set sail so fast----I thought I had at least 15 more minutes! I started trying to run to the ship, but my bum knee wouldn't allow it! I knew I had to get there within five minutes, or they would leave without me---because they wouldn't have even realized I was missing, probably, until the following day-----and I don't think they would have sailed back to get me at that point! I started trying to run, and HOP, yelling at the top of my breath "HOLD IT! WAIT! WAIT WAAAAAAAAAAIT". Finally as I got near the ship, the gangplank was gone and they were actually starting to sail! When they spotted me, screaming hysterically, they stopped and moved back against the pier. Then, one of the dockworkers said to me "OK----HOP ON"! I looked at him and figured he was joking! Then he repeated it "OK---HOP ON"! So I looked at him again, and he said a third time— "OK---HOP ON…. they're not going to put the gang plank back down, so you'd better hop on!" I looked at him again and said "WHAT??? You mean you want me to CLIMB over the RAIL???" "YUP! That's the only way you're going to get back aboard", he responded! That task would have been hard enough to do even if I were in GREAT shape! But to attempt it when I had a BUM knee was even more frightening! Anyway, I grabbed the rail and managed to kind of somersault over it, landing on the deck of the ship as I hoped to, but landing on my butt! Then, one of the other passengers (these freighters, in general, only take on about a dozen passengers), a real jerk, one of the guys that probably spends most of his time in the bar, said to me, as I lay on the deck still sitting on my butt, "DUHHHH.... see what you can DO when you really HAVE to???" In HIS mind, he probably thought he was complimenting me on this feat, but as I finally picked myself up and struggled back to my cabin, I was not very flattered by the 'compliment'!

THE CRUISE FROM HELL!

I've cruised on all kinds of ships----big ships, small ships, ferries, canoes, small freighters, Everglades air boats, paddle-wheelers. Nothing can beat the story of the time I took a small cruise ship to some offshore tourist islands. In order to protect the innocent (and the GUILTY!), I'm not going to tell you the name of the ship, nor the cruise company, nor the names of the destinations, nor the country, not even the CONTINENT where this 'experience' occurred, ---I'm just going to tell you what happened!

When the ship pulled into the bay where the first island to be visited was located, they had to use tenders because the bay was too shallow for the ship to enter fully. We knew about the need to use tenders in advance. The tenders were actually small motorboats which were attached to the cruise ship. When the ship reached the bay, it came as close as it could to the island, then it anchored and passengers boarded the tenders. All of a sudden, as the tender was getting closer to the pier, we felt a few bumps and the motor shut down. Apparently the water was so shallow that the motor's propellers began to hit the ground, and we were stuck about one half mile offshore. The water was so shallow that you could get out of the boat and walk around—the water was only about up to your knees. So the tender captain as well as several passengers got out to try to push the motor out of the mud, but they were unsuccessful. Other nearby motorboats used ropes to try to pull the boat, but they were also unsuccessful. We were not far from shore, and we were supposed to board a tour bus on shore to show us around the island. There was total miscommunication between the cruise ship and the tender, and finally the decision was made to send various local motorboats and dingys to transfer the passengers to shore.

However, there was complete miscommunication as to the tour bus we were supposed to board. Some claims were that the tour bus on shore would wait until all the passengers arrived. Other claims were that the tour was cancelled. Other claims were that the tour was cancelled but that the motorboats and dingys would take people to shore anyway so that they would be able to visit the island and browse the shops. In addition, claims were made that some boats and dingys would take people back to the cruise ship, while others would take people to shore. The boat that I got on never asked where we wanted to go, they just brought us back to the cruise ship. We were told that since the bus tour was cancelled anyway, we might as well go back to the cruise ship and that later on that day the cruise ship's additional tenders would take people back and forth to the island throughout the day. Later on that day, after returning to the cruise ship, I was told that the bus tour did indeed go ahead, but it was delayed by a couple of hours. Other sources denied that---saying-that the bus tour did not run at all. So what the true story was is still an unsolved mystery---like a "he said, she said"!

So, either I wound up missing the bus tour of the island because the boat returned me to the cruise ship, OR, because the bus tour was cancelled; it was ONE of those two reasons. Think THAT's "bad", huh? Well you haven't heard the rest of the story! The WORST is yet to come! After I and some other passengers were returned to the cruise ship, announcements were made that tenders would still be taking passengers back and forth to the island throughout the day. Every half hour, a tender would leave and shuttle people to the island, and every half hour that same tender would shuttle people back from the island to the cruise ship. In other words, the tender that brings passengers to the island would pick up passengers who already made it to the island and return them to the cruise ship. The only stipulation was that the LAST tender would be leaving the island at 4 PM and returning to the ship, after which the ship would sail away to the next island on the itinerary. I decided that, even though I missed the bus tour, I would still go to the island to browse and explore. At 2:30PM I boarded the tender and headed for the island. I was the last passenger to head toward the island. The tender arrived there at approximately 3:00 PM and dropped me off, while it picked up about a dozen people to return from the island back to the ship. When they dropped me off, they reminded me that the last tender back to the ship would be at 4:00 PM, and I should be on the pier by that time. I said that would be fine. (Remember, now, I was the last person they brought TO the island!) Anyway, I browsed around the island for about 45 minutes, then returned to the pier—about 15 minutes EARLY, just to be sure I was present when the last tender back to ship arrived! When it got to be 4:00 PM, I saw no signs of the tender, so I figured it might be a few minutes late—no big deal. 4:00 PM became 4:10 PM, and no signs of the tender! 4:10 PM became 4:20 PM---no signs of the tender! 4:20PM became 4:30 PM—still no signs of the tender! I walked around the pier and asked the owner of a small private boat if he saw any tender. He said "Yes", and told me it left about 20 minutes ago! I said that couldn't possibly BE, because I had been there almost one hour. Then he laughed and said he was just kidding. I laughed too, but the truth was I was in NO MOOD for jokes! This company already screwed me up enough for the day, making me miss the morning bus tour! So I waited and waited and waited some more. Finally, the harbormaster's boat entered the pier and docked, and I asked him if he knew anything about the last tender to the ship. He told me that the cruise ship, which was anchored offshore, already LEFT for the next island about a half-hour earlier. I started YELLING and SCREAMING, using all kinds of four-letter words and some additional explicatives! I told him that those assholes were supposed to send the last tender back to the shore at 4:00 PM to pick me up! He looked at his assistant and rolled his eyes----THEY were also summoned and involved with that cruise ship in the mishap that occurred that morning, when the tender got stuck offshore! The harbormaster telephoned the ship and told them that they stranded a passenger at the pier! After several calls, I told the harbormaster to tell them to turn back and send the tender to pick me up, which is what they were supposed to do in the first place! They refused to turn back but made a deal with the harbormaster for him to bring me in his boat and catch up with the ship, at which time I could board. I told them there would be NO WAY I would agree to that, because that would mean transferring to the ship farther out in the open sea, which is rather dangerous, and I can't swim! Their next idea was for me to go to the local airport and take a short flight to the next island, where I would meet the ship when they docked. I told them "NO WAY" again because I have a fear of flying ("flyophobia" as I call it!). I told them that if I did not have a fear of flying, that I would not be on this cruise in the first place, because I'd be traveling to more "way-out" places! Our final agreement was that I should stay overnight in a motel on the island, and the next day I could catch a ferry to the next island, and meet the ship there! I agreed, but to make matters worse, the harbormaster said that because this was the busy season (for tourism), he wasn't confident that I would be able to find a motel to spend the night. I had thoughts in my mind of having to spend the night on a park bench! Luckily I found –a motel to spend the night, and took the ferry the next day to re-unite with the ship, (and THEY paid all my expenses and gave me a few extra perks), but I missed the day at the next island because by time I arrived to meet the ship it was nightfall! They explained the mishap on someone calling out "PRESENT", (by accident) when they called out my cabin number, when they took roll-call upon sailing out the previous day! I guess we always have to find excuses for screw-ups---it's called CYA ("Cover Your

Ass")! We have to think *positive* though; the experience gave me this extra story to include in this book! Once in a while this company calls sends me brochures and promotions inviting me to take another cruise with them—a good marketing strategy! Unfortunately, the answer that I give them cannot be printed in this book—I tell them WHERE they can GO, and WHAT they can DO! (Use your imagination)!

PART V. Experiences with Cars, Car Services, Taxi Cabs, Car Pools, Limousines, Car Parking Lots

THAT'S OK, ------MY CAR IS BIG!

One summer, in the late afternoon, I planned to go to a summer music concert performed at a local community college. As usual, I was running late, so I called a local car service to take me there. The driver drove via Ocean Parkway, a fast-moving highway off limits to trucks and buses, which was quite congested with traffic. It was 'stop-and-go' traffic all the way there, and he was tailgating. I don't know HOW this particular driver ever got his license—must have won it in a raffle--- but he always seemed to be two inches from the car in front! Every time the car in front stopped suddenly, he always managed, somehow to stop without hitting it---maybe two inches away! After a few minutes and a couple of dozen times of putting up with this SHIT, I began asking him to slow down a bit—that is—not to tailgate the car in front of us. It was like talking to a wall! "That's OK, ------my car is BIG!" he kept responding, indicating he wasn't worried about crashing into the car in front because his car was bigger than most others. He didn't think that his car would suffer much damage if he crashed, because the car in front would get the worst of it! "YES, ---but my HEAD is not BIG", I kept responding, hoping he would get the message that I didn't care HOW big his car was---my head was much more important (I was sitting in the front passenger seat). When I'm running late for concerts, or, for that matter, running late for anything, I still call car services, just not THAT one!

"HEY MAN! THIS IS NEW YORK"!

I had to go somewhere (I don't remember where), and, as usual, I was running late! So I called a neighborhood car service, (which I believe is now defunct.) Anyway, they sent a driver who was relatively young (and STUPID!) ---probably in his late teens or early twenties.

This guy kept weaving in and out of traffic! He kept cutting off other drivers! Every time he cut someone off, they would open their window and give him the 'finger', and yell and curse at him. He would then yell back "Hey Man! —This is New York"! What he was trying to tell them was that since this was New York City, where everyone is EXPECTED to be arrogant, rude, and selfish, that they should have EXPECTED him to cut them off! This went on about a dozen times. At one point, a small pick-up truck with about five very mad guys looked at him, ready to beat the crap out of him (us???— 'guilty by association'?), and again, he responded "Hey Man---this is New York!"

Miraculously, I arrived at my destination, still in one piece!

THE GUANO ENTREPRENEUR (or) THIS STORY IS FOR THE BIRDS! (or) A BIRD IN THE AIR IS WORTH NUMBER TWO ON THE FACE!

I and two of my colleagues were walking home from work (school) one afternoon. We were science teachers at a high school and when often went home together by car pooling. Actually, that's not really accurate. We car-pooled in only one teacher's car, you might say we were just 'bumming' a ride. The teacher whose car we were using really didn't mind giving us a lift—he seemed to like our company. As we walked to his car, we used to throw the bull, talk shop, talk about crazy kids, crazy administrators and supervisors, and fellow crazy teachers!

Anyway, one day as we were walking and talking, one of my colleagues (one of us three) suddenly stopped short and said to me "Arg (a nickname he gave me instead of RJ), do me a favor, take a look at the side of my face, I feel something funny there".

I took a look and saw this long, greenish black strand of bird crap (feces) right between his temple and chin! Apparently, there must have been a flock of birds passing overhead which we didn't notice, and one needed to make a nature call, and my colleague's face happened to get in the way!

I started screaming "eeeeuuuuuuuuuwwwww"---eeeeuuuuuuwwwww ----eeeeuuuuuuwwwwwwww"! "You have bird crap there!" He said he thought it was bird crap, because it felt warm and slimy! "Do me a favor, get it off! Get it off! "Get it off"! he yelled. "Get it off HOW" I replied. "Don't you have a tissue?" he asked. I reached into my coat pocket and found a tissue. He didn't know this, and I wasn't going to tell him, but it was actually a USED tissue, one that I used previously and put back into my pocket to use again, if needed, after it dried.

"Yeah—I have a tissue in my pocket," I said. "Hold still and I'll wipe it off your face", I said. As I proceeded use the tissue to wipe the dung off his face, it started to SMEAR!
"EEEEUUUUUWWWW"! "EEEEUUUUWWWW"!
"EEEEUUUUUWWWW"! I yelled— "It's smearing"! Anyway, he asked me to keep wiping it off and when he gets home he will wash it off more with soap and water!

That was one day that was really for the BIRDS!

IN A PICKLE (or) **The Car with the Swiss Cheese Roof!**

I was returning home from my plot at the Floyd Bennett Field Community Garden one hot summer day and had to wait for the bus. I did not have a driver's license at that time, because some years earlier, shortly after I first received my license, I crashed into a city garbage truck and scraped the side of my car---so I had decided not to renew my license.

The bus I was waiting for was run by a private bus company rather than by the city. There are usually plenty of seats available on that bus, but on this hot summer day everyone was coming home from the beach, so the buses were fully packed, and the drivers would not stop to pick up more passengers because they literally could not fit in the bus! After waiting more than an hour and not being able to get on the bus, I began waving my fists at the drivers!

Realizing that it would be a long time before I would be able to get a bus, I decided to call a nearby car service. When the car arrived there was already another passenger inside---an elderly but feisty woman with several bags of groceries who obviously had just been shopping. I entered the car with my pitchfork that I used that day to till the soil of my (community) garden. I had the sharp prongs covered with some plastic and paper bags as a safety precaution., and I held the fork vertically, pointing it upward, so that if the car hit a bump in the road or pothole, and the forked moved suddenly, that nobody would get hurt.

For some reason, the driver stopped by the car service dispatching office before taking us home, and for whatever reason, the dispatcher told him to switch some passengers to another driver's car and to take on a few other passengers at the same time—kind of a passenger trade. I was told to remain in the same car, but he asked the woman with the bags of groceries to get into the OTHER car. Obviously, being a bit annoyed at having to switch cars (especially when SHE was in that car FIRST), she began to shout at the driver "you son of a BITCH!... You son of a BITCH!" As she began to exit the car, all riled up, groceries began to fall out of her bags---there were PICKLES (actually, cucumbers) all over the place, as well as some bananas, oranges, peppers, tomatoes, and a few other items! I helped pick them up and put them back into the bags. All this time she was CURSING at the top of her lungs! The driver didn't seem to quite 'get it'! He didn't have a CLUE as to why she was so ENRAGED! The other driver said, "Oh—looks like that woman is switching into MY car!". "You can HAVE her", the first driver replied!

When the driver finally reached my house and I was about to exit the car, I accidently moved the pitchfork upward, so that the sharp prongs pierced the bags that covered them, and they put some puncture holes into the ceiling of his car! He didn't see what happened. "OH SHIT!" I thought to myself---I just put some HOLES into the roof of this guy's car! While the prongs did not actually puncture the metal part of the roof, they DID puncture the cloth ceiling! I still wonder WHEN, and IF, the driver ever noticed that there were puncture holes in his car roof, and if he even had a CLUE as to WHERE the holes came from!

DOYLESTOWN, PA.----A NICE PLACE TO VISIT
(But I Wouldn't Want to Try to Hail a Caaaaab There)!

I had to get to a small town in Pennsylvania called Ottsville. Since I was not driving there, I was told to take a bus to the nearest larger town, Doylestown, and once there, I could get a cab or car service to Ottsville. Doylestown seemed like a nice place, but DON'T try to get a cab there! The only cab/car service had closed down about a year earlier, and there was no other taxi service in town! This may be hard to believe, but it IS what it is, (or WAS what it was)! To make matters worse, there are taxi services in nearby towns, but none of them would do pick-ups in Doylestown because they said they did not have the legal authority to do so, even though they knew the only taxi service in Doylestown was out of business. To make matters even worse, there were limousine services in nearby towns, but even they said they had no legal authority to do pick-ups in Doylestown! Finally, I walked into a travel agency and they finally convinced a limo service to do a pick-up in Doylestown (it cost me $200 for a round trip)! So while it might be a good idea to visit Doylestown, be prepared to do a lot of walking (unless a new taxi service has sprung up since the last time I was there—I believe it was in 2006).

THE PARTY LINE......IN A TAXI CAB????

I was in Albany, New York on some business, and stayed overnight at a hotel (the same hotel with the MUSHROOMS, explained elsewhere in this book)! I had to be at a meeting downtown at 9 AM, and, as usual, I was running late! I would normally take a city bus, but the ride would take at least 20 minutes, and it was already 8:45. Not that I would have lost the job if I were late, since the bosses knew me and expected me to be late (if I were on time they would have probably thought it was an imposter)! Anyway, I thought I'd take a cab to get there sooner, so I asked the hotel clerk to call me one. Well, it took almost 20 minutes for the cab to show up! If there weren't enough, before the cab showed up I saw the next city bus (which I would have been on!) pass right on by!

When the cab finally showed up, I felt relieved. I knew I would still be late, but maybe not THAT late! I guess I should have thought twice! As the cab drove toward downtown, the driver suddenly went off on a side road. I wondered why he did that, figuring he just decided to take a 'short cut' that he knew about. Turns out I figured WRONG! He stopped by a private house, waiting to take on another passenger! We waited for about five minutes for the guy to get in! When I asked the driver what was going on, he explained that this was "NOT New York City----cabs here do not take passengers one at time"! He explained that up there, cabs usually pick up several passengers at different locations and take them to different destinations, in the SAME cab. It reminded me of the old-fashioned telephone party lines!... (in other words, these were the cave-men days)!

It was bad enough that I had to wait a few minutes until this next guy got into the cab, but to add insult to injury, I saw him, through the window of his house----he was browsing through and reading some of his

MAIL that he hadn't opened from the previous day! He took his sweet time before getting into the cab!

FINALLY, he got in and we were on our way! Of course, the driver dropped the other guy off at HIS destination BEFORE he headed towards mine! To add more insult to injury, there were problems with the cab's cooling system, and it began to overheat and steam began BILLOWING out of the engine BEFORE we got to my destination! The driver flagged down another cab who took me to my destination. There was no additional fare, but I 'had' to (in MY mind) give TWO tips! When I finally arrived (about half an hour late versus ten minutes late had I taken the city bus!), I wasn't sure if I should explain my lateness, figuring nobody would believe the story anyway, but I DID----at least it would give them a laugh!

THE "P"

I was entering a supermarket parking lot in my car when another car had stopped and was in my way, blocking me from entering further. I blew my horn to get him to move. He was waiting for another car to move out so he could get that parking spot, and he was not budging. So he continued to ignore my horn. I had no problem at all with him getting that spot; I don't even like to park in that area because it is too close to the entrance and space is sparse and maneuverability is difficult. All I wanted him to do was to back up a bit so I could pass. Well, he continued to ignore my horn, and I was stuck on the side of him. Within a few seconds, cars were in front of and behind me, and I was sandwiched-in between them. So I figured "the hell with this" and pulled into the first spot I saw, which was the spot this jackass was waiting for (the previous car had just pulled out completely). Again, I did not want that spot, but because the jackass wouldn't back up a bit to let me pass, I had no choice but to take it to get out of the way of the other cars. When I came out of my car, he was complaining that HE was waiting for that spot before me. "I know", I replied, "but you wouldn't let me pass you, and because of your arrogance I was sandwiched-in by other cars in front of and behind me, so I just pulled into that spot as soon as the other car left". We continued to argue and I tried to explain that it was his own arrogance, by not letting me pass, that caused me to pull into that spot (of course, I could have then pulled out of the spot and given it to him, but when someone's being a real JACKASS, we know where they can go)! I told him that the next time he's blocking the road, and someone wants to pass, not to be such as asshole and just backup and let them pass! He then drove away to find another parking spot.

When I came out of the store about one-half hour later, I put my packages in my car and began to exit the parking lot. Since there are stop signs and traffic lights in the area, it can take five or ten minutes, maybe even longer, to finally exit the lot. As I'm waiting, suddenly this same guy comes over, out of 'nowhere', and starts banging on my front, rear, and side windows with his hands and fists (he must have left the parking lot and was waiting for me to come out). For about two minutes, that idiot banged on my windows, knowing that I couldn't come out of the car with other cars in front of and behind me. Then he ran away through an alleyway! Lucky for him, because I wanted to kick his ASS! If the guy had a problem, he should have confronted me face-to-face, instead of banging on my windows and running away. We have a name for a coward like that, a "P"! So, you may ask, "what does the "P" stand for?" Some will say the "P" stands for "PUNK"; well, maybe. But there is another word that the "P" might stand for-----I'll leave it up to YOU, the reader, to figure this one out!

ANYONE FOR CHESS?

I recently went on a two week cruise to Hawaii that sailed round trip from San Diego. I stayed in a motel in San Diego for a couple of days after the cruise and decided to visit the San Diego Zoo, which is reputed to me among the best in the world. (And it was a great experience)! Anyway, I first went to Motel's front desk and asked them to call me3 a cab to take me to the zoo. They told me it would be necessary for them to call because cabs are usually lined up on the street out front.

When I went out front, I saw an empty cab, with two people playing chess on the hood of the trunk! They actually had a chess board on top of the trunk hood! One guy was the cab driver---I didn't know who the other guy was. Playing CHESS on the HOOD of a taxi cab---QUITE STRANGE! I walked over and stood behind them for a few minutes, figuring they would notice me and realize I was a potential customer, but that didn't happen. They were unfazed---didn't even FLINCH! ----really into the game! I felt guilty to interrupt and ask for a ride because I didn't want to disturb their game! I walked another block and saw another cab— windows open but no driver! I realized that the missing driver was the OTHER guy playing chess with the driver of the first cab! I cleared my throat a couple of times, then they noticed me and took me to the zoo. I apologized for messing up their chess game! When I left the zoo and was looking for a ride home (back to the motel), AGAIN---cabbies playing CHESS on the hood of their cabs! That's one thing you'll never see in New York---cabbies playing chess on the trunks of their cabs! This was the first time I felt guilty for patronizing a cab driver!

TWO 'PUTZES'

It was a quiet Sunday afternoon, I, my friend and his wife, and another couple were walking in the neighborhood and stopped at the crosswalk, waiting for the light to change. The street had two lanes, one for both traffic directions, separated by a solid white line at the center. Cars are not supposed to cross the solid white line, and U-turns are absolutely illegal, but drivers make them anyway, since they rarely get caught or ticketed.

As we waited for the light to change, we noticed two large cars, possibly limousines, one behind the other, waiting to make an illegal U-turn as soon as traffic was clear. Something about this scenario seemed strange, because both cars seemed hesitant to make the turns. My friend said "Uh-Oh—let's wait a while—let's not cross yet because I have a feeling something's going to happen".

Both cars belonged to car services (different companies). What we expected to happen was that the car at the front would make the (illegal) U-turn first, followed by the car behind. However, the car up front was still hesitant to make the turn (WHY I don't know!) The driver of the car behind probably got tired of waiting for the front car to make the turn, so he decided to turn first instead. Apparently, the driver of the front car got annoyed that the car behind was making its (illegal) U-turn first, and he decided "NO! That's NOT going to HAPPEN!" So as the car behind started making its U-turn, the front car also started to make its U-turn, going around the car behind at the same time as it was turning and actually went partly onto the curb in order to 'beat' the behind car's complete U-turn! As this was happening, all of a sudden we hear "SCREEEEEEEECH!" ---the front car scraped the side of the behind car as both were competing to be the first to complete the U-turn! An elderly Asian man was standing by the bus stop and also saw the whole thing! He BURST out laughing "Ah-ha-ha-ha-ha-haaaaaaaaaaaaa"! I wanted to laugh also but was afraid that the drivers might hit me. Both drivers got out of their cars and started arguing, yelling, cursing at each other! I, my friend and his wife, and the other couple went home their separate ways. I was laughing all the way home, hysterically! People who passed me by on the way must have thought I was 'nuts'! Later on that night I phoned my friend and asked him what he thought about the incident. His response was, "those guys were TWO PUTZES!". Right he was, and hence the title of this incident!

PART VI. My Experiences on Elevators

THE 'SABBATH' ELEVATOR THAT DIDN'T ONLY WORK ON THE SABBATH! (or) The 'Wanna-Be' Elevator Operator!

When I was about 10 years old, my aunt and uncle lived around the corner from me in Brooklyn. Huge high-rise apartment complexes were being built in the Brighton Beach/Coney Island area, and in the mid 60's, when they were completed, my aunt and uncle decided to move into one of them. They rented an apartment almost on the very top—on the 22nd floor, and, of course, the only way to get up and down was to use the elevators. They even had two sets of elevators, for odd and an even floors. Besides loving to ride the elevators, I had another 'hobby'—pushing all the buttons for all the floors! That would be great if the elevator was filled up and there were 'customers' for EVERY floor, but if only a few people came on, they would have to stop at EVERY floor, since I had pushed all the buttons. That means that a ride that should normally take only about two minutes NOW would take almost TEN minutes!

One day this young couple got on the elevator near the top floor to go downward. I entered first on the top (22nd) floor, and of course, pushed ALL the buttons, so everyone inside now had to stop at every floor! Regarding this married couple, the husband apparently was impatient to get to the ground floor, and was FURIOUS at me for pushing all the floors! Every time the elevator stopped at a floor, he got more and more pissed, and I laughed! His wife tried to calm him down, trying to explain that I was just a kid having fun, so that he shouldn't PUNCH me or something! But as the elevator landed at each and every floor, he became more and more pissed, and I tried to hide the laughs as best as I could! If you could picture him, in your mind, getting madder and madder when it stopped at the 18th floor, then the 16th floor, then the 14th floor…... imagine how PISSED he was by time it reached the ground floor! Anyway, when it reached the ground floor, and the door opened, I ZOOMED out, probably at the speed of light!

---

* A Sabbath elevator stops at every floor, on the Sabbath, for Sabbath observers.

THE *HOLY* ELEVATOR (or)
The Incident That Happened but Might Not Have Really Happened?

The next story is not what I would call "funny", but it is so strange that I'm including it here. If you think it should not be included, remember what I told you earlier about the tail not wagging the dog!

Anyway, I was in a hotel in the Catskills, upstate New York, riding an elevator. The elevator was rather crowded, and we were going downward just a few floors, like from floor 4 to floor 1. On one of the floors we stopped at, several people were waiting to enter. When the door opened, two of the people waiting to enter were a woman, probably in her 70's, with a friend, another woman about the same age. As the elevator door remained open, and just before boarding, this woman put her hands around her chest and SCREAMED out "JESUS"! She said it so loud and forceful that I got scared, or at least shocked, for the moment! Her friend looked at her, (and I looked also) and she whispered to her "WHAT????" Then the woman spelled it out "J, E, S, U, S", kind of whispering, to her friend. Both her friend, and I, looked at her mysteriously, then her friend and I looked at each other, mysteriously, wondering what that was all about! Everybody else in the elevator car was quiet through all this, not uttering a word!

So what actually happened there? Did this woman have some kind of holy "vision"? Her friend acted as if she never expected anything like that from her, as if she never saw her act like that before!

What I found really weird was that after the elevator got to the first floor, and everybody exited, NOBODY said a word about this, as if the incident never happened! It was as if everybody in the elevator was pulling a 'Sergeant Shultz'! This causes me, after witnessing the whole thing myself, to question whether it really happened at all! While I was there and KNOW it happened, I often question whether it really DID happen? Could I have been hallucinating????????

"SUSAN SMITH…… STUCK IN ELEVATOR"

First, let me say that Susan Smith might or might not be the person's real name---it may be a fictitious name that I'm using to protect the innocent. So just WHO is Susan Smith and what the heck does she have to do with a story about an elevator? Well, let me now explain.

Susan Smith is a TV newswoman. I watch her very often on the morning news on a local station. One morning she was not on the show, and I (and I'm sure MANY viewers) were wondering why! All of a sudden, a sub-title starts appearing on the bottom of the TV screen, "Susan Smith……stuck in elevator". This message appeared many times throughout the broadcast! I don't know all the details, but apparently, on her way to work that day, she got stuck in the elevator and couldn't make it in to work. And I think I heard later on that firemen had to be called to get her out! While you may feel that's NOT a funny story (and I AGREE---it could be quite scary), what I did find 'funny', if not 'very odd', was the way the TV station posted the information (below the screen by a sub-title) to its viewers! Why did the station have to be so honest? Couldn't they just say something like "Susan Smith is off today"? Couldn't her replacement just mention that a few times, rather than the station posting it, over and over again, with sub-titles?

Anyway, while I do like Susan Smith, and still watch her broadcasts, and feel she is a great newscaster, I would someday like to see her in person so I can be my usual obnoxious self and point at her and say…..." HA! HA! YOU got STUCK in the ELEVATOR!"

PART VII. Fast-Moving Animals

THE RIDER'S TURN TO JUMP

It was the early 70's; I was in college and my best friend was in community college. We lived near each other, so we often went places together---movie theatres, concerts, basketball games (mainly to watch the cheerleaders), etc. One day he recommended a horse show, I think it was in Madison Square Garden, but I don't remember exactly. It was some kind of show where horses are trained to jump over hurdles with the rider. I'm not really a horse show fan, but he was enthusiastic about it (by word-of-mouth), so I agreed to go along.

Basically, the show was just watching horses and their riders jumping over hurdles. It was the same crap horse after horse after horse. I found it quite boring and had to watch that 'crap' for about two hours! I was also a bit pissed because I felt that the horses were being exploited by their riders---that they were trained to do these tricks just to make money. So, after the first hour or so of boredom and being pissed, I turned to my friend and said "I hope the fucking horse kicks the fucking guy off!" (It wasn't that I wanted the rider to get hurt, but I said it just out of boredom and frustration). About 10 seconds after I said that, the horse and rider approached the hurdle, got ready to jump, but for whatever reason, the horse got spooked and stopped short. As the laws of physics will tell you (an object in motion remains in motion), you can probably guess what happened. Instead of the horse jumping over the hurdle, the rider went flying over it, landing, luckily, on his rear end! Everybody in the audience yelled out "OOOOOOOOOOOOOOOH"! Luckily, the rider didn't seem to be hurt, but he probably wasn't going to be sitting for a while! My friend, in a state of disbelief, turned to me and said "You SCHMUCK! You say something and it HAPPENS!"

I guess the moral of this story is to be careful what you wish for---- you may get it!

DOG DAY MORNING

When I was a kid, I always wanted a dog. When I was twelve, my parents finally agreed to let me have one. We picked one up from an animal shelter, a five month old female spaniel-setter mix, already named "Pal". I played with her a lot, and, as you can probably guess, teased her a lot as well!

Sometimes, after playing with her and teasing her, she would "go berserk"! She would start barking and running all over the place, her eyes bulging outward, tail bent inward, running around the house from room to room, back and forth, barking wildly, sometimes crashing into furniture, and finally jumping onto the couch. Then she would quickly calm down and jump off the couch, as if she had to do that to get it all out of her system! I never quite understood that scenario, but I thought it was quite entertaining. Was this just a way of letting off steam from her excitement? A way of getting it out of her system? I honestly don't know.

Anyway, one day my aunt (Pearl) stayed over our house for the holidays, and she slept on the couch. The next morning, while she lay on the couch, I wanted to show her this new 'trick' I taught my dog (the dog 'going berserk'), so I played with and teased her until she 'went berserk' again. I and my aunt watched in amazement as she started barking wildly and running all over the place. My aunt, still laying on the couch also thought it was entertaining, and she smiled and laughed. Now, remember I told you that the "show" ends with her jumping on the couch? Well, it ended the same way again, with the dog jumping onto the couch, but this time my aunt was still laying on it! So the dog jumped literally right on top of her! You should have heard the "Wooooooooooooooooooo!" she yelled out. I think she kind-a got the wind knocked out of her for a few seconds! After that, she never again asked me to show her any new 'tricks' that I taught my dog!

A BIRD IN THE CAGE IS WORTH TWO ON THE FLOOR!

When I was a kid, I had a few parakeets as pets. One day I decided I was going to 'scare' the birds, so I moved the cage onto a small table. I was going to throw a small pillow onto the cage, which I figured would just bounce off it and scare them. So I threw the pillow at the cage, but, not being good in physics, I miscalculated the results. Instead of just bouncing off the cage, it knocked the cage down! I shouted "OOOOOOPS!", and I ran over and picked it up! The birds were not hurt, but YES, there were SCARED! My mother made me sweep up all the bird seed, and some other 'stuff', which was literally, ALL OVER THE FLOOR!

PART VIII. The Impromptu (or) Stories that really don't belong in this book, (but which I'm adding anyway!)

The *Wikipedia* definition of Impromptu is "a free-form musical composition with the character of an *ex tempore* improvisation as if prompted by the spirit of the moment......" *The Free Dictionary* defines impromptu as "prompted by the occasion rather than being planned in advance" and "spoken, performed, done, or composed with little or no preparation. *Dictionary.com* defines impromptu as "suddenly or hastily prepared, made, etc.". So basically, an impromptu is something just 'thrown in' at the spur of the moment, just by the whim of the thrower. The following stories have nothing to do with subways, buses, or other forms of transit, but since I'm the 'boss' here, and the tail does not wag the dog, I'm putting them in anyway!

"F-I-R-E" IN THE CROWDED THEATRE!

My friend and I went to a movie theatre (the extent of my social life during my college days!). I don't remember the name of the movie we saw (I guess it really made a good impression!) but it started out with a scene about cavemen finding a TV set and trying to figure out what it was and how it worked. Apparently, there was some kind of technical problem with the projector or with the film reel itself, because the film kept stopping (freezing) and starting several times and each time it stopped it took a minute or two to be fixed. I think you know what happens—people in the audience start yelling every time the film freezes! It seemed as if somehow the film kept jamming in the projector.

After several freezes and fixes, there was a scene where the cavemen were trying to start a fire, as usual, by rubbing two sticks together. Of course, the film kept jamming and freezing again, and at one point it froze during the scene where the sticks were being rubbed together. This time, however, the projector operator apparently couldn't unjam the film, and it actually began to melt and caught on fire! We actually saw, on the screen, the FLAMES appearing! This was no camera trick nor optical illusion! The heat produced in the projector by the film being stuck literally set it on FIRE, and the audience saw the flames projected onto the screen! Boy, this is what you can really call a "hands-on" approach! It was not 'virtual reality'--- it was more like 'LITERAL REALITY'! I've heard of movies using things called "Sensurround" and "Smell-o-Vision", but WHAT would you call THIS---"Flame-o-Vision"???……" Fire-o-Scope"???

THERE'S A FUN-GUS AMONG-US! (or) Wild *MUSHROOMS* Couldn't Drive Me Away!

I was doing some consulting work in Albany, New York and was staying at a relatively nice hotel, where I've stayed a number of times before. I was told that the hotel was under new management, but that didn't really matter to me. When I entered the room I was given, I noticed something odd on the floor near the window. It looked like some kind of decoration, or brick-a-brack; it looked like a model of a bunch of mushrooms. "Gee, that's interesting!", I thought to myself, "but why would they put a decoration like that on the floor, right on top of the carpet"? I wondered if this was the hotel's idea of being "fancy"? So I touched it and realized that this was no "decoration"! They were a bunch of real mushrooms growing out of the carpet! Nearby was a wet towel. Apparently rain leaked in through the window over a period of time and the carpet constantly got wet. They probably put the towel there to dry it up (obviously it didn't work well!)

I know mushrooms grow in moist soil, but never knew they would grow in a hotel room out of a carpet! Were they using the wool of the rug as a food source, or the wooden floor underneath it? I also knew that if I told anybody about this, they wouldn't believe me! So the next morning I bought one of those disposable cameras and took pictures (shown below)! MUSHROOMS, anyone????

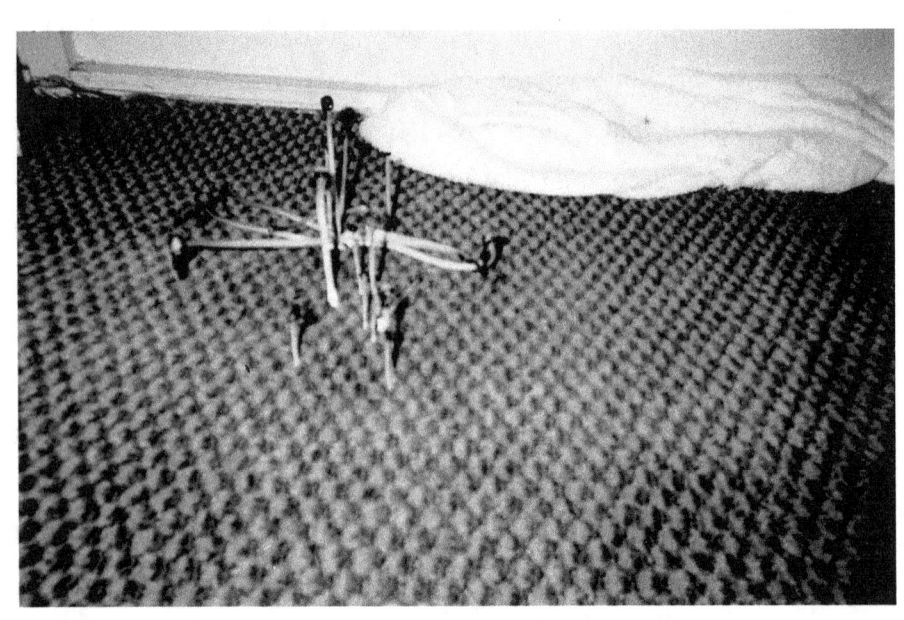

NO SENSE LAUGHING OVER SPILLED MILK!

I don't know when I became such a wild, 'problem' child, but I'm sure it started when I was very young, most likely, a toddler.

I remember one day when I was about five years old, several relatives came over. We were all sitting in the living room, watching the repairman fix our black and white TV set, when my uncle asked my mother for a cold drink. My mother was always dropping things on the floor, and I would laugh! Anyway, my uncle followed my mother into the kitchen. She opened the refrigerator door to show him what cold drinks we had. I remained in the living room watching the repairman fix our TV set---these mechanical/electrical things always mesmerized me! All of a sudden, I heard a noise "Bump…………...BUMP-BUMP…..Bump…..BOOM!" I knew something fell out of the refrigerator. "Ooooo-oooooo-oooooo", I yelled, hoping to see what fell so I could laugh! I ran into the kitchen as fast as I could (the HELL with the TV set!), and saw my mother and my uncle looking at a bottle of milk, spilled all over the floor! I immediately burst out laughing at the top of my lungs, hysterically!---"ah-ha-ha-ha-ha-haaaaaaaaaa!" My mother, knowing me, just ignored it, but my uncle started yelling at me: "what's so funny?"

To this day, even as I write this story, I burst out laughing, hysterically, just remembering it!

PAYBACKS ARE A (son of a) BITCH! (or) Boy, Cigarettes are sure Getting EXPENSIVE!

I was waiting on line in a bank one day; the line was long and moving slowly and the waiting time was at least 20 minutes! This man, after waiting all that time, goes to one of the tellers and cashes a check. I don't think the check was very large, and maybe the teller was running short of small bills, so in the transaction she gives him a one hundred dollar bill with the smaller bills. He walks away mumbling and cursing, (in an accent) "HUNDRED DOLLAR BILL"! "How I going to go into store and buy pack of cigarettes with HUNDRED DOLLAR BILL? ---You SON OF BITCH"! Actually, I wanted to tell him that with the rising price of cigarettes today, it may not be long before you'll NEED to use that hundred dollar bill! On the other hand, maybe this incident was a message from the 'Universe' that he shouldn't smoke!

SNAP, CRACKLE, POP!

I was in a movie theatre with a friend one night---that was the extent of my social life for many years! As we were watching the movie, and everyone was quiet, I heard a noise and suddenly felt my seat move downward, as if one of the screws fell out or one of the axles broke! My friend looked over at me and I looked at him, both of us wondering what happened. For a couple of seconds, it seemed as if the entire incident was over with, whatever the heck it was, when suddenly, the seat collapsed downward some more! My friend looked at me again, and I looked at him again, and, as before, it seemed as if the second incident was over with. SUDDENLY, the seat collapsed a THIRD time, and I was still in the seat, but it was on the FLOOR, so we knew it couldn't collapse a fourth time! I just sat there, on the seat, which was on the floor, saying absolutely NOTHING, wondering what, if anything, would happen NEXT! I sat there, both of us looking at each other, probably for the next 30 seconds or so, when my friend began to laugh hysterically! Then, after another couple of seconds, people in the back and sides of me began to laugh HYSTERICALLY also! I just SAT there, motionless and expressionless for a couple of minutes, laughed also, then I got up and we both moved a few seats way! My friend said the reason it was so funny was because of the WAY the seat collapsed---in three steps: "boom-----boom------BOOM!".

THE LAUNDRY MAT FROM HELL!

When I was kid, we had a washing machine in our basement, which usually worked pretty well, but once in a while it broke down, and until the repair-man showed up, which might have been a week later, we had to use the laundry mat. At this laundry mat, once in a while someone put too much soap powder in the machine, and suds would overflow out of the top of the machine (the soap dispenser). If that weren't enough, there would be so many suds coming out of the machine that the person using it would have to stop the machine, open the door, and remove the clothes. When this happened, the suds and the wash water went literally all over the floor, and the person who caused this flood would then have to mop it all up! I used to LOVE that! I got HYSTERICAL watching these people mop up the entire laundry mat floor! They would be mopping up the floor, and I would be standing there laughing, HYSTERICALLY, at them! Sometimes, they would see me laughing, and they would get hysterical too!

WHO PUT THE "BREAK" IN BED AND BREAK-FAST? (or) Who Put the Bomp in the Bomp-Ba-Bomp-Ba-Bomp?

I periodically have to go to Albany, New York to do some consulting work, usually during the summer months, and it requires staying overnight at a hotel or motel for a several days. It so happens that a few years ago, when I had to go, the BAR exam was being given there that week, so all the hotels and motels were booked solid, several months in advance. This was a special problem in my case, since I book things at the last minute! Anyway, I finally managed to get a room, but it was in Schenectady, New York, a suburb of Albany, which was only about a forty minute bus ride away. The room was in a "Bed and Breakfast"—that was all I could find (and it my FIRST time in a Bed and Breakfast)! I stayed there a few days. It wasn't exactly my 'cup of tea', since I am used to hotels and motels, but I was happy to get at least THAT! The woman who owned it was very nice and she had two nice dogs that I enjoyed petting and playing with (and sometimes TEASING)! In my room, there was a large, beautiful chandelier above my bed. One morning, as I was sitting on the side of the bed putting on my shirt, lifting my arms up to get the sleeves in place, I felt a contact with something and heard the sound of a sudden, CRASHING noise! I couldn't imagine what happened! The owner came running into my room to find out what happened. What actually happened was that the chandelier, apparently, was hanging a bit too low above my bed, and as I had put my arms up to get the sleeves in place while putting on my shirt, I guess I hit the bottom of the chandelier! I broke a few of its glass ornaments, and they wound up all over the floor, and most did not actually break—the glass was still intact! The owner was concerned about whether I was hurt, but luckily I was not. A woman who was also staying there heard the commotion and came in to find out what happened. She noticed that one of the ornaments had rolled into the hallway, and she asked the owner if she could keep it as a souvenir!

I was apologetic and asked if it could be fixed, but the owner was more concerned about whether or not I was OK. I assured her I was. Of course, after I left, I was HYSTERICAL! I was 'cracking-up' about it all day!

WHY DIDN'T MY GRANDPARENTS LIKE ME?

I never knew my paternal grandparents but my maternal grandparents lived until my early twenties. I always felt that they didn't really like me, but never understood why.

Maybe THIS, as only *one* example, might solve the mystery. One night my grandfather came over to 'baby sit'. I was about ten years old. We had an old TV set in my basement which he was watching, while I, *supposedly*, was watching TV in the living room. I stood on the top steps of the staircase and starting shooting rubber bands toward the back of his head. Apparently he didn't know I was there! When one finally hit the 'target", he must have thought it was a fly or mosquito because he yelled out a shout and 'swatted' the back of his head with his hand! I quietly ran back into the living room in case he realized what really happened!

WHY DIDN'T MY GRANDPARENTS LIKE ME (II)? (or) Opening Up a Bag of Worms!

When I was about 9 years old, I had pet birds, alley cats, goldfish, tropical fish, parakeets, finches. My grandparents were 'snowbirds', traveling to Florida (Miami Beach) in the winters to escape the cold New York weather. I had the impression that Florida was loaded with lakes and swamps and oceans full of tropical fish, so I kept writing to my grandfather asking him to catch me some and bring them home when they return in early spring. (I had no idea that he never went fishing a day in his life)!

Anyway, his sister (my grand aunt) went to visit them in Florida for a couple of weeks, and when she returned she told me that, yes, my grandfather went fishing and caught me a "BIG BIG RED FISH", and that he was keeping it in his bathtub until they were ready to come home. I actually BELIEVED her! Then, I thought, "Gee, if he's keeping that fish for me in his bathtub, he's gonna need FOOD for it!". IT was now early Spring here in NY, and the trees were LOADED with Tent caterpillars! "AHHHHH" I thought to myself, THAT'S THE SOLUTION to the problem! So I gathered up about a pound of the caterpillars, put them into a plastic bag, squished them up so they couldn't escape, and MAILED it to them!

When my grandmother answered the door bell, it was the mailman with my package, and it was ninety cents POSTAGE DUE (equivalent to about nine dollars in the early 60's)! Not knowing what it was or who sent it, she paid the ninety cents. When she opened up the plastic bag, she almost passed out from the smell! MY parents NEVER heard the END of that! Moral of the story: Never tell a lie (my grand aunt) to a child, (ESPECIALLY "RJ")!

WIENER-SCHNITZEL
(Pronounced "Veena-Schnitzel")

When I was about six years old, my parents rented a bungalow in Kiamesha Lake, N.Y., part of the Catskills. This area is sometimes called the "Borscht Circuit". There was another six year old kid who lived in the bungalow colony, whose name was Ivan (not his real name, but close). Anyway, the other kids used to tease and make fun of him, maybe because he was short and had a lot of freckles and curly hair. They called him "Wiener- Schnitzel". They and I teased him constantly, calling him that name, and he always got really pissed! He would say "I'm IVAN---NO Weiner-SCHNITZEL!!!" The more pissed he got, the more I would call him that! Anyway, one day he got so pissed that we got into a fight. I was always good at starting fights, but the truth was, I couldn't fight for SHIT! (Probably still can't)! Needless to say, I got my ass kicked! (I'm sure some of you readers are saying "GOOD")! But I got my revenge! The next day, we were both on the playground on the swings. The first thing he said to me was "Hey---do you remember the BEATING you got yesterday?" I didn't answer him. A few minutes later, one of my shoes fell off as I was on the swing. He laughed "Ha-ha-ha-ha-haaaaaaaaah-ha----RJ's shoe fell oooooofffffffffff"! I got pissed, but I didn't want to fight him again, realizing I'd probably get my ass kicked again. So I got off the swing, put my shoe back on, turned around, and PUSHED him off the swing! He ran home crying to his mother! I went home, laughing, telling my mother what happened, and she said "that's not nice"!

Mmm-Mmm GOOD! (or) Doing the Can-Can (or) The Soup Kitchen

When I was in first grade, the teacher asked us to bring in food for a food drive for the needy. Only canned foods would be accepted. I brought in a can of soup, in a paper bag, being the generous kid I was!

A couple of months later, the teacher gave me back the can of soup, still inside the paper bag. I don't remember why she gave it back, but apparently there was some problem—maybe it was expired—I really don't remember the reason.

It so happened that the day she gave it back to me, the class went to the auditorium to rehearse for a play. The teacher was busy setting up the stage, so she seated the class in a few rows of seats nearby in the audience area. All of a sudden, and for no reason, this classmate (I'll call him "Ricky") starts pushing me! I asked him why he pushed me but he kept mumbling something, and pushed me again! I yelled out to the teacher, who was busy on stage, but she just responded "just a minute". Ricky pushed me again, so again I yelled out to the teacher, who again responded "just a minute". Ricky pushed me again, and again I yelled out to the teacher, and again I heard "just a minute". Then, again, Ricky pushed me, but, rather than repeating the above scenario, I picked up the bag containing the can of soup and whacked him over the head with it! He began to cry. Then the teacher (who I should name "Miss Just-A-Minute") finally came over, and asked what happened, so I explained it to her. She yelled at me for hitting Ricky over the head and I told her he kept pushing me for no reason and that I kept calling her but she wouldn't come over. She made me feel the bump on Ricky's head, at which point I responded "I'm sorry"! Well, needless to say, Ricky never pushed me again after that!

PIPE DREAMS (or)
The Corn Cob Pipe from Hell!

I am a cigar smoker, but once in a while I smoke a pipe, often a corn cob pipe. One winter day I was visiting my aunt and uncle in Florida, and I entered a store which sold cigars and pipe tobacco, and noticed they had some corn cob pipes. These pipes were unlike any other corn cob pipes I had ever seen before, because they were MAAAAAAD BIG! I never knew corn cobs could ever be so big and wide, but these sure were! So I bought one and some pipe tobacco and lit it up. As I was walking in the street and smoking the pipe, I noticed something rather odd. It seemed to be a very hot smoke! Yes, corn cob pipes can reach high temperatures when being smoked, but this one was REALLY hot! Wondering why the heat was so intense, I took it out of my mouth to examine it, only to see that the entire bowl with the tobacco was burning! Burning on the OUTSIDE as well as the inside! The entire bowl of the pipe was in FLAMES, literally! I shook the pipe and threw it on the ground. So ended the case of The Corn Cob Pipe from Hell! It would have probably been better for me to invest in a regular wooden pipe, at least on that occasion!

QUIET in the Theatre! (or)
The Human BOOMerang!

I was visiting my aunt and uncle in Florida and one day I decided to see a movie in the local matinee. In New York City, the theatres are 8usually quite large, and the rows of seats are very long. In Florida, at least in the theatres I've been in, the theatres are relatively small and the rows of seats are not that long.

I'm sure that most of us have experienced what it's like to enter a dark theatre after the movie has started. The lights are out and it's very dark. It takes at least a few minutes for our eyes to adjust to the darkness. At the same time, we usually start walking through the row of seats even though we can't see the people sitting there, hoping we don't step on too many feet or fall into someone's lap!

Anyway, I started walking through the row of seats, as carefully as I could so that I would not step on anyone's feet, or trip and fall into their lap, if there were anyone already there! Luckily, there were few, if any at all, people seated there. But what I forgot was that the theatres in Florida were not that large, and the rows of seats not that long, so I kept walking through the row of seats until I heard (and FELT!) a big "BOOM"! What happened was that I crashed right into the wall! To make matters worse, the walls in that theatre were hollow, so I really caused a big sonic BOOM when I hit! I was unhurt but felt really STUPID! I looked around, quite embarrassed, figuring people would start laughing at me, hysterically, but, strangely, they were so engrossed in the movie that I don't think they even noticed the sonic BOOM that I caused!

THE HAPPY JUROR

I was called for jury duty one day and the lawyers were in the process of picking a jury from a large group of potential jurors. I think this selection process is called "impaneling", or something like that. One by one they called us up and asked us various questions. Everyone seemed to answer to the best of their ability, and as honestly and sincerely as possible. After questioning the entire group, about 15 people, the lawyers would tell those who were picked to stay and the others would be 'excused'. One by one they continued to call us up to ask us questions. They eventually called this young woman, probably in her early twenties, and she instantly BURST OUT LAUGHING as soon as they called her name! "Ah-ha-ha-ha-ha-ha! Ah-ha-ha-ha-ha-ha! AH-ha-ha-ha-ha-ha"! This continued for about five minutes! You could see the lawyers were getting annoyed, even though they had no idea what she was laughing about! Everyone in the room looked at each other in DISBELIEF! What the hell was so funny??? After this five minute rant, she apologized and explained what she was so hysterical about. It seems that a friend of hers, also in the potential juror group and sitting next to her, told her "I bet they'll call you up next", and just at that instant, they called her! Apparently, she found that HILARIOUS!

Needless to say, she was NOT picked to serve on that case!

WITHOUT EVEN THINKING! (or) The Case of the 'No-Brainer'

And speaking about juries and jurors, I was with a group of potential jurors being interviewed (impaneled) for an accident case where the victims were suing for damage to their car. One by one, people were called on and asked numerous questions pertaining to their ability to serve as impartial jurors on that case. There was this one guy who they called on and was asked what he did for a living. He responded that he was some kind of automobile damage appraiser for the transit authority, so that when cars or buses get into accidents, hios job was to examine the cars and assess the value of the damage. The lawyers then asked him if his job would in any way interfere with his ability to serve on that case, since it was a case involving a car accident and vehicle damages. He said it would not interfere, because he was an expert in that field. He then said "I can make a decision WITHOUT EVEN THINKING!" I was cracking up all day! Imagine-----having a juror who makes decisions without thinking!

Needless to say, he was NOT picked to serve on that case!

TOMATO WARS! (or)
Like A Scene From 'Animal House'!

When I was a teenager, I had a friend, I'll call him "Tim", who lived 'almost' next door to me. What I mean by "almost next door" is this: We lived on a block of attached brick houses, but we all had backyards. He lived not directly next door, but one house away from next door. From my backyard to his was a distance of about 20 feet. Anyway, Tim was a 'wild' kind of kid—always getting into trouble, although minor trouble---stupid little things. We used to get into little fights—fights over stupid little things—as they say "boys will be boys"! Some of the fights we used to get into were Animal House type "food fights". We would throw things—usually food items at each other and into each other's back yards! We would throw things at each other like tomatoes, potatoes, cantaloupe rinds, eggplants, peppers. Every time one threw a food item, the other would duck down or run to avoid getting hit. Once, during a food fight, I threw a raw egg at Tim while he was on his porch, and he opened his door to try to run into his house, but just as the door opened the egg hit it, almost smashing the glass! These are the kinds of fights we used to get into! These foods fight didn't occur every day, but just once in a while. Tim also had a swimming pool in his back yard, and sometimes the food item would land in the pool, making a big splash!

My family was not on the friendliest of terms with the neighbors (a woman and her mother) next door on the opposite side, while Tim's family was very friendly with them.

One summer day I was talking to Tim about who remembers what, and he was eating a piece of fruit, I think it was a slice of melon or cantaloupe. When he finished, he threw the rind into my neighbor's yard, the neighbor between my house and his house. I was relatively friendly with that neighbor, and I even used his yard to grow some crops. So when Tim threw the melon rind into their yard, I was mad, and took it personally! So, in retaliation, I went in my house and grabbed a tomato, and threw it into his yard. Then he got mad, and threw a tomato into my yard. Before you knew it, another 'FOOD FIGHT" ensued—this time it was mainly a 'TOMATO WAR'! Anyway, this war went on for about ten minutes; I threw a tomato at him, he threw a tomato at me, and it went on and on and on! Anyway, remember I told you that I didn't get along with the neighbors next door to me (on the opposite side of Tim's house). Well, it so happens that on that particular day at that particular time that me and Tim were having our TOMATO WAR, the neighbors that I didn't get along with (the woman and her mother) were sitting on their porch in their backyard, sunning themselves. They saw that Tim and I were involved in a TOMATO WAR but they didn't seem to notice or care—they were not fazed by it. Anyway, as the war was going on, Tim threw a tomato at me, but instead of just landing in my yard, it hit the wire fence between me and the neighbors, and it SPLATTERED---all over them!

They screamed "OOOOOOOOOOOOH!", and they started to clean themselves off. And WHO do you think got yelled at??? WHO do you think they SCREAMED at???? Well, remember that those neighbors were friendly with Tim's family? So they certainly weren't going to blame TIM! So I got the blame for the entire thing! Even though it was Tim who threw the tomato that hit the fence and splattered, it was I that got blamed! They didn't say a word to TIM! I told them that TIM threw that tomato, so they should yell at HIM, not me! But they pulled a Sergeant Schultz---made believe they didn't even see Tim---that it was ALL MY FAULT!

'BA-DA BOOM' IN THE BOTANY LAB!

When I was an undergraduate in college, many many 'moons' ago, I took a botany course, which had a lecture session and a laboratory session. At the beginning of the lab there was a one hour "recitation" section, in which the professor lectured about the lab experiments that we would be performing on that day. During that lecture, all the students were seated around the laboratory tables, listening, asking questions, and taking notes. We were all seated, not in regular chairs, but rather on stools. You had to be very careful when sitting on those stools, because if you start to twist or turn or lean forwards or backwards it could fall (and you along with it!). Anyway, one day the professor was lecturing and the entire class was very quiet—you could hear a pin drop! All of a sudden, we hear a giant "BOOM"! Some guy, apparently, was leaning backward on his lab stool and must have leaned just a little bit too far—and "BOOM" ---the stool fell over, with HIM in it! What happened next was even more interesting: the whole class looked over to see what happened; the professor looked as well—for three seconds---and then went on lecturing as if nothing had happened! It seems that even the BOTANY PROFESSOR was pulling a Sergeant Schultz! Luckily, the guy didn't get hurt, but he surely was Maaaaaaad EMBARASSED!

GET OUT-A-HERE KID YA' BOTHER ME (II)! (or) My Audition as a Replacement for 'Dennis The Menace'!

Many of you are probably wondering about my reasons for writing this book and the way that my mind works! That's understandable! I often wonder about myself! Well, maybe this story can answer your query.

When I was a kid my mother sometimes went to the big department stores in Manhattan. She took me with her, probably not because she wanted to, but most likely due to the fact that she couldn't find a babysitter, or more likely because no babysitters would sit for me!

I couldn't stay still while she shopped and browsed, so I would roam around the floor. I remember once when some woman was walking around the floor carrying a Siamese cat on her shoulder. I would tease the cat, making faces at it. The woman got mad, understandably, and, although she didn't SAY anything, she began to stare at me with a mad look on her face and followed me around the floor. I didn't run, but started walking away quite quickly! What's funnier is that a few minutes later, I saw another kid do the SAME thing—and she began following HIM!

As I walked around the floor, I saw a man doing a demonstration with a blender, which we now refer to as "food processors". He would be at a podium showing how the blender worked, and he was surrounded by interested potential customers, maybe about 20 or 30 or so, all of whom were women and whom might be interested in the gadget for home use. He would put food—usually fruits or vegetables—in the blender and turn it on at different speeds, faster and faster. Then he would tell them that they should NOT put the blender at the MAXIMUM speed, because it would overflow and SPLASH all over the place! He then asked them if they actually wanted to SEE THAT! Everybody yelled out" Nooooooooooooo"!

But I yelled out "YES! YES! YES!" Of course, the guy just ignored me, making believe he didn't hear me and that I was not even there! I guess HE was the FIRST person I met to 'pull a Sergeant Schultz'!

CONCLUDING REMARKS 1 (or) R.J.'s Final Thought!

Well, I hope you enjoyed the stories—all are TRUE----that I wanted to share with you in this book! I promise to keep tabs on things that occur from this point on so that I can put them into the 'sequel'.

Like I stated in the *Preface*, anyone can write a book of this kind—about the crazy, exotic experiences they have experienced or witnesses on subways, buses, cruises, tour buses, elevators, and the like. It's just a matter of putting your experiences to paper, or computer files.

Throughout this book, I made references to the fact that many people who also witnessed these occurrences sort of said or did nothing, that they just did not want to get involved. This was evident in their making believe that they did not see or hear anything—that they were just 'oblivious' to the situation---that they just didn't want to get involved!' That is why I have coined the expression "pulling a Sergeant Schultz". I'm confident that Sergeant Schultz, played by the late John Banner in the 1960's series "Hogan's Heroes", is the one who made believe he did not see or hear or know anything that was going on that wasn't 'acceptable". His famous words were "I see No-THING, No-THING!" and "I know No-THING, No-THING"! This was evident in the Kitty Genovese murder case, as occurred in Kew Gardens, Queens, New York City on March 13, 1964. As described by Wikipedia, Kitty Genovese was a young woman murdered by a killer who came back a second time, to finish the job, and nobody—none of those who heard or witnessed it—intervened or called the police. This has often been called the "Bystander Effect" or the "Genovese Syndrome" ---basically all those who heard the commotion or witnessed the crime "pulled a Sergeant Schultz"! They saw N0-THING, No-THING, they heard No-THING, No-THING, they knew No-THING, No-THING, they DID No-THING, No-THING! One thing that I am hoping for is that the expression that I coined in this book, "pulling a Sergeant Schultz" will become a 'new expression'. I think you kn ow what I mean by 'new expression'---words and expressions that pop up over time and become part of the English language, even 'unofficially'---words and expressions like "dis", "right-on" "rock-n-roll" "disco" "hip-hop" and many others. One thing about these new words and expressions that they all seem to have in common is that nobody seems to know WHERE these words came from, not WHO actually coined them! My hope is that "pulling a sergeant Schultz" will become another one of those new expressions. If that happens, we will ALL know who coined it, the one and only R.J. Nobleman, and WHERE the phrase was coined----"SORRY FOR THE INCONVENIENCE/GOING YOUR WAY"!

PART IX. MORE CRAZY STORIES

"We Fell in KAHCKEY!" MORE CRAZY BUT TRUE STORIES

When I was about 7 years old, there was a large vacant lot ("the lots") around the corner. Kids on the block used to go there to play all the time. People also brought their dogs there to do their 'business' (if you know what I mean!). Anyway, there were two kids (brothers) a few years younger than me on the block, and they also liked to play in the lot. The lot had grasses and weeds all over the place, and you always had to look carefully where you walked to avoid stepping on anything hazardous or from falling into a hole. One day, I saw the two brothers walking home from the lot, and they had all kinds of yellow and brown sludge-like material on their clothes, arms, hands, and even on their faces. "We fell in KAHCKEY", they said to me! For those readers who do not know what "KAHCKEY" is, it is the street name for dog feces. Well, all I can tell you is that their mother did not let them play in the lots anymore after that! And I'm glad that I did not have to help clean them off!

Doin' the Bumble Bee Boogie!

My next door neighbors' back yard was always a big mess! They never mowed their lawn or cut their grass---the weeds grew sky high, especially during the summers! Neighbors were always complaining especially if they had hay fever. Finally, we convinced them to hire gardeners.

One day while the gardeners were working, we saw them suddenly begin to jump up and down like crazy, and they began to run all around the yard, yelling and screaming at the top of their lungs, and we couldn't figure out why. Then we found out. Apparently, there was a bee hive on the ground, but the weeds were so tall that they couldn't see it! As they walked, obviously they stepped on the hive! The bees apparently were not too pleased with that, and decided to let them know it! To me, the scenario looked like they were inventing a new dance---the "Bumble Bee Boogie" ---all that was still needed was someone to set it to music and add the lyrics! It could possibly be the latest new dance craze!

The 'Pizza Rat'!

I was walking to the subway station in lower Manhattan, on my way home from my college teaching job. They were doing construction on the streets and gutters, as happens in NYC very often. There were construction crews with jack hammers and cranes all over the place, with non-stop noise. There was a pizza place on the corner, and since it was early Fall and relatively hot, its doors were left open.

Suddenly, a giant rat crawled out of the sewer, obviously due to the disturbances caused by all the construction. You could see that the rat was scared out of its wits!

It didn't know if it was coming or going, and was looking for a place to run and hide. Guess what----it decided to run into the pizza place, since the open doors were an open invitation. I saw it run inside--and I KNEW what was going to happen next! As I passed by I heard AAAAAAAAHHH! AAAAAAAHHHH! AAAAAAAAAAAAAAAAHHHHHHHHHH!

Customers were yelling and screaming, running all over the place! It was like a scene from a HORROR movie! People were trying to hit the rat with their umbrellas (it rained earlier that day)! I witnessed the entire event as if it were in slow motion! I became hysterical! I entered the subway station hysterical! I boarded the train hysterically! People on the train did not know what I was laughing about--I'm sure they thought I was nuts! But in New York, I'm sure they weren't surprised! Too bad I didn't know how to capture it on my cell phone---it would have gotten millions of views!

A SHIRT OF MANY COLORS!
("GEEEEE, THANNNNNNNKS!")

When I was about 10 years old, I was still a SLOB! I hardly ever washed my hands or face, I used to spit on the floor, I often picked my nose and rolled the buggers (cootsies) between my fingers, I would sneeze and wipe the snot away using my sleeves, among other 'slobbish' things! One day, one of my teachers in an after-school program told me "YOU are the worst slob ever! You are annoying, disgusting, you have no manners and no class whatsoever! I've never met a 'SLOB' or PIG like you among the many students I've ever had in my classes" Then he continued to berate me (actually, it was not "berating me since it was the TRUTH!) for about another ten minutes! After he finished berating me, he became silent, waiting to hear what my response would be. My response: "GEEEEEEEE! THANNNNNNNNNNKS!". In the bible, there is the story of Joseph, who was famous for having a coat of many different colors. As the SLOB I was that I spoke about above, one day I came to class with a shirt of many colors---but NOT because it was designed that way, but rather because whenever I ate, I would wipe my fingers and hands on the nearest available 'napkin', which was usually my SHIRT! So when I came to class (late, as usual), all the other kids were hysterical and began to tell me, like the teacher, what a SLOB I was and how 'GROSS' and DISGUSTING my shirt was! Rather than acknowledge that they were right, I tried to tell them that this was a new style of shirt, ---a new design----and that I actually bought the shirt that way! Believe me, they did not BUY that explanation!

"DO YOU HEFF *ELEPHANTS* HERE??????"

I was on a cruise to Alaska, and like all cruises, when we stop in a town passengers usually go on local tours. On one tour we were taken to a local marketplace. We saw booths selling ivory-made items and souvenirs, and one guy on our tour, a real GENIUS, who came from a foreign country where there obviously are elephants asked the tour director, upon seeing all the ivory for sale, "Do you heff ELEPHANTS here????" The tour director had to explain to him that they did NOT have elephants there, but that they did have walruses, with TUSKS, which was where they get the ivory from. Regarding the inquisitive tourist, it just goes to show how STUPID some people can be!!!!!!

THE SUN, GRRRRRRRRRRRADUATION, AND 'BIG MIKE'!

When I taught high school science (biology, chemistry, and Earth science), I always liked to tell jokes. Most of the jokes were not really funny, and most were also very 'CORNY'! 'Big Mike' was a student in my class—kind of a GIANT! He must have been 6 foot five, and weighed about 300 pounds! He had a friendly, jolly personality, and always laughed at my jokes, not only to get a passing grade, but also because he had a great sense of humor, even when my jokes were corny (which was almost ALL of the time!). When he laughed, the entire building SHOOK—like there was an earthquake! The entire building trembled when he laughed, and his laugh could probably bust your ear drums! I think he might have had to stay an extra term before he could graduate in order to make up some missed classes. I loved having him in my classes, because he 'livened and spiced them up, so that the other students would not fall asleep (and probably so that I WOULD NOT PUT MYSELF TO SLEEP AS WELL!).

One day, in Earth science, I was covering the unit on astronomy, and I was discussing supernovas (exploding stars). I taught that all stars eventually burn out their hydrogen fuel supply, and die out, usually by exploding (a supernova). After exploding, all that is usually left behind is a cloud of gas, called a "nebula". Sometimes, out of this nebula, new, smaller stars are born. And I noted that all stars are actually suns, and all suns are actually stars, our sun included! I explained that, as a typical star, our sun will probably also explode some day, forming a supernova, but that scientists tell us that it will probably not happen for another 4 to 5 billion years or so. That means that the sun, and our planet and solar system, will still be around for another 4 or 5 billion years, and then "CAPUT"! I then asked the students if they should worry about that, since 5 billion years is kind of a LONG TIME from now! All the students raised their and said "NO" when I asked "how many of you are going to worry about that?" Then I made one of my corny jokes, by saying "well, you SHOULD worry about that, and when they asked "WHY?", I responded, "Because that's just about the time, that MANY of you, if not MOST of you, if not ALL of you, will be GRRRRRRRRRADUATING!!!!", and I said that in a high pitch, as I generally do when I tell my jokes! (Although I'm not sure if it was really a "joke"!) 'BIG Mike' got the joke right away, and began his ear-drum' blasting laugh! The building began to SHAKE---and everyone in the building knew that it was NOT an earthquake, it was just 'Big Mike' laughing at one of my CORNY jokes!

"RJ, YOU HAVE A *WAY* WITH BIRDS!"

One summer I was taking a two-week field course called "Arctic Ecosystems" in Churchill, Manitoba, Canada, which is known as the polar bear capitol of the world! While we did spot some polar bears in the distance, we never got too close to them to be in any real danger. The professors (about 4 of them) always guided the students in the field with rifles, just in case we accidently stepped over a polar bear resting in the bushes (in the Willows).

One day, while the class was walking through the fields, we spotted a large, black bird on the branch of a nearby tree. The bird was about the size of a crow. I was munching on an apple at the time, and decided I would hold the core part in my fingers and held it up to the bird (who was about 20 feet away on the branch), just to see what, if anything, the bird would do (in other words, whether the bird would fly near me to try to get the food). Upon seeing the apple core, the bird, unexpectedly, flew toward me, and landed in my chest and face! It happened so fast that I didn't even realize what happened, and I held on to the apple core; then the bird flew away! Another student, seeing this said "RJ, you're SUPPOSED to let it (the food) GO! But, like I said, the bird flew into my face so fast that I didn't have time to react! Then the other student said "RJ, You have a *WAY* with *BIRDS*!" I was hoping the bird would return to get the apple core, but it flew away instead! So I tossed the apple core away in the field. Who knows---maybe there are now several apple trees growing there!

THE MALICIOUS, COMPULSIVE LIAR!

When I was about 11 years old, and in the sixth grade of elementary school, there was a kid about my age in one of my classes, ---we'll call him "Humphrey". Humphrey wasn't exactly my enemy, but he wasn't exactly my 'friend' either. But one thing I will say about Humphrey, he was a compulsive liar, and often a malicious liar as well! I remember one day when he rolled up a big spitball and threw it at the teacher while the teacher was sitting at his desk. The teacher did not actually SEE Humphrey throw the spitball, but he saw it come from Humphrey's direction. So he asked Humphrey, in front of the whole class if HE threw the spitball. Humphrey adamantly DENIED throwing the spitball, saying "I didn't throw it---I SWEAR, I SWEAR, I SWEAR---I didn't throw it!" But the teacher was convinced that Humphrey DID throw the spitball, and the dialog went back and forth several times, with Humphrey denying and SWEARING he didn't do it! Even Humphrey's best friend, seated next to him, testified that before the spitball was thrown, Humphrey showed it to him and asked him "Should I THROW it? ---should I THROW it?" (With BEST friends like THAT, WHO needs ENEMIES????). Anyway, the scenario ended there, as the teacher couldn't absolutely prove that Humphrey threw it (though he and I were SURE that he did!).

Anyway, one day, during lunch break, when me and another classmate (a friend of mine) were walking home (we were allowed to go home or lunch), I saw Humphrey walking across the street. I yelled to my classmate, loud enough for Humphrey to hear "AH HA HA HA HAAAAA---THERE'S HUMPHREY, THERE's HUMPHREY, AH HA HA HA HA HA!!!". There was no malice intended, I just wanted Humphrey to know that I saw him across the street. Humphrey didn't respond, he just went on his way walking home, and we went on our merry way----the incident (I thought) was over!

When we returned to school about an hour later, me and my friend were in gym class, playing games and whatever. All of sudden, a student monitor approached me and told me that someone was waiting outside the gym and wanted to talk to me. I had no idea WHO it was, but I went out the door to find out. Who was there? It was the PRINCIPAL, accompanied by Humphrey. And Humphrey concocted some crazy story that during lunch-break, as he was walking home from school, me and another kid saw Humphrey across the street, and we started THROWING ROCKS at him! I told the principal that no such thing happened, and that I merely saw Humphrey across the street, and since I knew him, just yelled out "AH HA HA HA… there's Humphrey, there's Humphrey", and that NOBODY threw any rocks at him! The conversation ended there. But to this day, I still wonder why Humphrey concocted such a story! I guess that it will just be one of those 'Unsolved Mysteries'! After that incident, I just kind of completely ignored Humphrey, although in high school he was in some of my classes again. LUCKY ME!!!!!!!!

"RJ" -as- "GW"

We all know the story of the father of our country, George Washington. Now, I'm not trying to compare myself to George Washington, but we did have one thing in common---our decision not to tell a lie!

We all know the story that George Washington chopped down his father's cherry tree, and when is father asked him about it, he said "Father, I cannot tell a lie---I CHOPPED DOWN THE CHERRY TREE!" Supposedly, his father was so proud that his son told the truth (there were no daytime talk shows with lie detectors in those days!), that he didn't punish George.

My father smoked cigarettes—the non-filter ones, although he didn't seem to inhale them. He used cigarette lighters to light them up—the old fashioned kind with flints and the liquid lighter fluid cans that you had to often refill. One day, when I was about 6 or 7 years old, I decided to take the cigarette lighter apart, just to see what it looked like inside. I wound up DESTROYING the lighter, and I even burned it up! It wasn't because I didn't want him to smoke (the cigarette scare didn't happen yet---this was back in the 50's)). I just wanted to see what it looked like inside and how it worked. After I destroyed it, I threw it away, thinking my father wouldn't even miss it because he had a few of them. Apparently I was wrong! He did miss the lighter, and began looking all over the house for it. He had my mother help him search for it, and he even asked ME if I saw it—to which I answered "NO"! After A couple of hours passed and him not finding it, I finally ADMITTED that I took the lighter apart and destroyed it! I realized I would probably get a spanking, so I decided to try using psychology on him. I told him how sorry and ashamed I was that I took and destroyed his lighter, and as he was contemplating giving a spanking (with his BELT!), I said to him, "Daddy, you BETTER HIT ME!", showing him that I was sorry for doing it and at first LIEING about it! IT WORKED!!!! He was so happy that I finally told the truth that he didn't spank me! So while I'm not comparing myself to George Washington, I definitely see a bond between us!

Wahhhhh! Wahhhhhhhh! Wahhhhhhhhhhhhh! I Lost My Coot-sie!!!!

Ever since I was a kid, I loved to pick my nose! Even more fun for me was to roll the bugger between my fingers! If I didn't drop and lose the bugger, I could roll it for HOURS--it was great fun! In those days we did not call them "buggers" .... we called them "coot-sies"! And with all that nose-picking, I was always getting nose bleeds--once I even ad to have my nose cauterized to stop the bleeding, but I didn't let that stop me! The kids in school used to call me "Bugger-nose Joe" --even though Joe was NOT my name! Anyway, one day I picked a giant coot-sie and went around the corner to sit on a relative's stoop, where I rolled and rolled the coot-sie-- probably for almost an hour, and had maaaaaad fun---until I dropped it and it got lost! I panicked! "Oh no---I lost my coot-sie"! When I realized it was lost, I started to cry--"how could I lose my coot-sie?"!!! I ran home crying to my mother "Wah! Wahhhhh! Wahhhhhhhhhhhh! I Lost my coot-sie", I explained to her! I continued crying uncontrollably! Finally, in an attempt to console me, she picked out her own coot-sie from her nose, and said," HERE! ---here's a coot-sie!". That me cry even louder! "NO---I want my OWN cootsie!", I screamed! Eventually my crying stopped---I realized tomorrow would be another day! As the saying goes, "another day, another coot-sie!".

Fountain-Pen-Pete ----meets---- Bugger-Nose-Joe!!!

As I previously explained, when I was a kid, I loved to pick buggers out of my nose and roll them, for as long as possible, between my fingers--usually between my thumb and index fingers! The kids in elementary school nick-named me "Bugger-Nose-Joe", even though "Joe" was not my name! Anyway, in my class there was a kid who I'll call "Bob". Bob was a kid who always came to school dressed maaaaad nice! He always wore a clean, pressed white shirt and a tie---sometimes even a sport jacket or suit! Obviously, he came from a well-to-do family. In contrast to Bob, I was a total SLOB! Bob also always wrote with a fountain pen---which I felt was kind of odd! So I gave him the nick-name "Fountain-Pen-Pete", even though "Pete" was NOT his name! And every time I called him "Fountain-Pen-Pete", he would call me "Bugger-Nose-Joe"! So if "Bob" ever happens to be reading this, I hope he remembers that HE is the real "Fountain-Pen-Pete"! Will the REAL "Fountain-Pen -Pete" PLEEEEEEASE stand up?".

JACK in the Box?????
NO!......JIM in the Box!

We all remember, as young kids, we often heard the tune "All around the mulberry bush, the monkey chased the weasel.... POP goes the wea-sel! Well, when I was a teen, I had two friends that lived nearby. One was Jim,---quite a character, quite a prankster, always getting into trouble, and me into trouble along with it! Then there was my other friend, Jerry, not quite a prankster, was the kind that people used to play the pranks on! On day, Jerry told me he was coming over, and I told him we would hang out on my back porch-- we could sit in the rocking chairs and throw the bull. Jim saw me and also wanted to sit and throw the bull as well, so I told him "fine", because Jerry was also on his way over. Being a good prankster, Jim got a great idea! He told me he would hide below my porch until Jerry arrived. Then, while me and Jerry were rocking, throwing the bull, he would continue hiding under the porch, and after a few minutes, Jim would "POP" up---just like a Jack in the box, just to see Jerry's reaction! So when Jerry rang my doorbell, Jim hid under the porch as planned, and me and Jerry sat there in the rocking chairs throwing the bull for about 10 minutes. Then, suddenly, Jim "POPPED" UP, silently, with his arms spread out, and with a BIG GRIN on his face! It took Jerry a few seconds to notice what happened, and suddenly, Jerry screams out "AHHHHHHHHHHHHHHHH!!!!! "---as if he saw a ghost! To this this day, I am still cracking up about it!

ONE FISH, TWO FISH......MY FISH, YOU FISH!

I and a friend, call him Jerry took a bus trip up to the Catskill mountains, a resort area in Swan Lake, NY, known as the Borscht Circuit----with many hotels. We took a mile or two walk with our fishing gear, even though I'm a vegetarian and do not eat fish. (But any fish I were to catch I would feed to my dog. Anyway, the fish weren't biting too well, and he did manage to catch one fish, which he placed in his bucket. Horsing around like we always do, I said to him "You see that fish that we caught in that bucket......? That's MY fish!" To which HE immediately replied "NO!... it's MY fish! Then I immediately replied, "NO!... it's MY fish!" To which HE immediately replied "NO! It's MY fish!" This went on and on for about ten minutes---all the while we were just joking around. A fisherman on the other side of the pier overheard us and must have thought we were serious, and was afraid we would erupt into a fight. "He reached into his bucket (in which he had already caught about half a dozen fish). And said "HERE!!! HERE's a FISH!" And upon that, he took a fish out of his bucket and placed it in OUR bucket! We thanked him and laughed to ourselves, not telling him we were just kidding around, or he might take the fish back! (On after thought, I should have said to Jerry "Ya' see those TWO fish in the bucket? ----they're BOTH my fish!).

Why You Should NEVER Keep Keys in Your Shirt Pocket!

One day at work, I was using the John. I had my set of keys in my shirt pocket. These included my house keys, car keys, keys to my safe and file cabinets, keys to various rooms and closets at work, my safe deposit box keys, and other important keys. The set was relatively heavy, consisting of at least a dozen. When finished, I bent down to flush the toilet and the set of keys fell out of my shirt pocket just as I flushed! "O SHIT!", I said to myself---looks like the whole set was just flushed away! "UH-OH---what am I going to do NOW????" I thought to myself! Luckily, because of the laws of physics, the set was too heavy to get flushed! So when I looked, I saw that they were saved from being lost forever! That was one time I didn't mind reaching into the bowl and pulling them out! Of course, I washed my hands and the set of keys with BLEACH right after that! Lesson learned: NEVER keep keys in your shirt pocket, especially when using the John!

ALL GASSED UP!

A friend of mine, let's call him Jerry, used to visit every night, and we used to sit on the front stoop and throw the bull for a couple of ours. My basset hound, Axelrod, would sit on the side and just rest. One day, I said to him, "SHHHHHHH" be quiet---do you hear THAT?" We all remained silent for a few minutes. He looked quite puzzled, because he didn't hear anything (and truthfully, neither did I!) Then, all of a sudden, I laid a giant FART----so loud that you could probably hear it a block away! Then Jerry exclaimed---"Uh-oh! ---the DOG is DEAD"! (Actually the dog did JUMP-UP in fear!). Anyway, that was the start of our future "FART FIASCOS"! After that, every time he came over, and we sat at night on the front stoop, it sounded like a ship was in the harbor, blowing its' horn! Sometimes it was HIS ship, sometimes it was MY ship! II wonder if the neighbors were able to get any sleep!

TPP---"THE PHART PHONE!"

Speaking again about farts, my friend Jerry and I used to call each other often, just to throw the bull. One day during the conversation, I came up with a great idea! As we were talking, I said to him "QUIET" ---- SHHHHHHHH! ----did you hear THAT?" He said---"WHAT? Did I hear WHAT?" I said "THAT----did you hear THAT?" Again he yelled "WHAT?" ---did I hear WHAT?" "THAT!" I said again ---did you hear THAT?" Again, he exclaimed "WHAT?!!!" Then I put the phone receiver against my butt and let out this giant F-A-R-T! So now the "Phart phone" (NOT the "Smart phone") was invented! After that time, every time we called each other, we took turns farting into the phone! So whoever is reading this story, please consider this a new venue when talking over the phone to friends or relatives (or to telemarketers during robocalls!) Just be careful to use discretion---for example, I wouldn't do it when talking to prospective employers or 'high-society" folks, nor clergy members!

MUFFLED EARS, X2!

I was on a week-long cruise, from Vancouver to Alaska. I shared the cabin with 3 other men, none of whom knew each other. Cabin sharing was common to lower the cruise prices, but were usually intended for passengers who knew each other. I am a loud snorer, and one guy really couldn't handle my snoring. So during the night when I snored, he would get out of bed and shake my arm, to wake me from snoring. While this did work, it didn't work for long—maybe an hour or so. So all night he had to repeat this over and over. I apologized for my snoring, but didn't have much (if ANY) control over it.

Another time I was sharing a cabin at a camp which converted to a one week getaway. Again we had to share a cabin, 2 to a cabin, and we did not know knew each other. Again, my snoring was, horrendous, like a ship blowing its horn before sailing off ("ALL ABOARD")! This time, in order to wake me to stop my snoring, the other guy would blurb out SCREAMS during the night! Again, I apologized but told him it was uncontrollable, as I have sleep apnea! The next day I heard the guy talking to a friend, thanking him for the ear-muffs! "Thanks a million" he said! "The ear muffs really helped! I was finally able to get some sleep!".

The LEAST Stupid Teacher!

When I was teaching high school, I, like most teachers, always wondered whether the students appreciated me. One class I was given consisted of kids who recently came here from other countries, and spoke very little English. To make matters worse, the class was filled with kids from countries all over world, not just one, so it was like teaching in the United Nations! It was a class filled with kids speaking 20 different languages! On top of that they were quite rowdy, and that's an UNDERSTATENENT! One possible reason was that I liked to horse around with them--- as you can probably imagine. The following year, at the next level, the class was taught by another teacher, let's call him Mr. Jones--- one who liked teaching non-English speakers! These were called ESL (English as a second language) classes, but he was much more serious and did not joke around, so the kids hated him---because he didn't stand for any nonsense! One day a few of these former students saw me in the hall, and said hello (plus a few other things—as you might imagine!). When I asked them who their new teacher was, one kid replied "Mr. Jones----he's a more stupid teacher than YOU!" Another student added "he's a much more stupid teacher than YOU!" Another kid added he's a HUNDRED times more stupid teacher than you!" Finally, another one of those geniuses shouted "Mr. Jones is TEN TOUSAND TIMES more STUPID teacher than you!". I know I should have felt bad, being 'DISSED' by my former students, but actually, I took it as a COMPLIMENT---that there were other teachers "TEN TOUSAND TIMES more stupid teacher than me"! So I went walking through the halls, smiling! When other teachers asked me why I was so happy, I just told them that I was just thanked and complimented by my former students! It just proved to me that kids really DO appreciate their teachers after all!

WATCH OUT FOR THOSE 'ROBOMECHANICS'!

One morning, while driving to work, the sun's angle caused the light to hit me right in the face. I couldn't see more than two inches in front of me. Apparently, there was a van directly ahead of me, and was stopped for the red light. I jammed on my brakes but "CRASH" ---it was too late! There was some mild damage to the back of the van, which my insurance company fixed, but I had no collision insurance for my car, since it was quite old. My front grill was busted up, but the radiator wasn't damaged, and the car was still drivable. The only problem was that the hood didn't close all the way and the front grill was busted. Rather than investing money to fix up my jalopy, I just continued to drive it. One day shortly thereafter, some guy stops his car and said he wanted to talk to me. He told me he worked in an auto body shop and the he had a rubber hammer with him and for ten dollars, he would bang the dents out my hood, and that he could do it right then and there, and it would only take ten minutes. I was reluctant to allow a stranger to do this, but with all his fast-talk, I thought "what the heck", paid him the ten bucks, and watched as banged out the dents. My front right headlight, had also been broken, and he told me that for another sixty bucks, he could buy and install a new headlight, but he would have to order it first and needed the sixty bucks now, and that in one week he would have it and meet me in front of my home (nearby), at which time he would install it. Since he did a good job banging out the dents in the hood, I fell for his story (like a JERK!) and paid him the sixty bucks in advance. One week later I stood in front of my house, waiting for the swindler to show up with the new headlight. I'm STILL waiting (this was about six years ago)! I guess P.T. Barnum was RIGHT----"there's a sucker born every minute"! In this case, the sucker was ME!

Why You Should NEVER Keep Keys in Your Shirt Pocket!

One day at work, I was using the John. I had my set of keys in my shirt pocket. These included my house keys, car keys, keys to my safe and file cabinets, keys to various rooms and closets at work, my safe deposit box keys, and other important keys. The set was relatively heavy, consisting of at least a dozen. When finished, I bent down to flush the toilet and the set of keys fell out of my shirt pocket just as I flushed! "O SHIT!", I said to myself---looks like the whole set was just flushed away! "UH-OH---what am I going to do NOW????" I thought to myself! Luckily, because of the laws of physics, the set was too heavy to get flushed! So when I looked, I saw that they were saved from being lost forever! That was one time I didn't mind reaching into the bowl and pulling them out! Of course, I washed my hands and the set of keys with BLEACH right after that! Lesson learned: NEVER keep keys in your shirt pocket, especially when using the John!

YOU'RE BURNING THE CEILING!

My father was almost an amateur handyman, always finding things to do to fix up the house. Sometimes he needed my help lifting and carrying things around. One day the light bulb blew out in a small bathroom we had in the basement. You might think replacing the bulb would be a simple job, but the basement was relatively dark, so e asked for my elp. E wanted me to hold the flashlight on the bathroom ceiling while e screwed in the new bulb, but we could not find the flashlight, so he asked me to hold up a candle so he could see what he was doing. As the candle burned, he began to unscrew the old bulb and screw in the new bulb, all the while I held the burning candle up to provide light. All of a sudden he yells out "You're BURNING the CEILING"! What happened was that as I was holding up the candle, (I guess I held it up a little too high), the flame started torching the ceiling!!! Even today, many years later, the ceiling around the light fixture has a permanent black (carbonized) scathe mark around it to commemorate the occasion!

LET'S FIX THE LIGHT -----SNAP"!

On another occasion, in another basement location, another light bulb burned out, but this time, screwing-in a new bulb wouldn't work, because the entire light fixture was broken. So My father bought a new fixture--- it was small, maybe 5 inches in diameter, and made of porcelain. He asked me again to help him screw the fixture onto the basement ceiling, while he held it in place manually. Using the screwdriver, I turned it and turned it and turned it, but the screw kept turning—there was no end! He asked me to be gentle, but I told him it wasn't necessary to do it gently because the screw kept turning and turning and turning. Finally, as I continued to turn the screw, we heard "SNAP!" The porcelain base of the light fixture broke apart! So I went back to the hardware store to buy another one---laughing HYSTERICALLY all the way!

TWO's COMPANY (THREE's OK TOO!)

I was on a cruise ship—I think it was to the Caribbean, and to save money, I took a guaranteed share, where they find another passenger to share your cabin. The guy that they found was about my age, and single. On night, as I was nearly asleep, the guy returns with a girl he met. He must have thought I would get out of bed and leave the cabin for a couple of hours, so I would let nature take its course. NOTIHNG DOING! I just went back to sleep while they made out (and whatever else!). If he wanted to do that, let him book his OWN private cabin next time!

RESERVATIONS FOR TWO! (OR) "SWITCH-TRACKS"!

I called a car service to pick me up because my car was in the shop (my old jalopy---which was in the shop most of the time anyway!). When I went outside to wait for the car to show up, I noticed my next door neighbor get in a car before I did. Obviously she must have called car service about the same time. I just assumed (NEVER "A_S_S_U_M_E"!) that HER car service showed up first, and I would just wait for MY car service to arrive. I waited and waited for about 15 minutes, then another car service (NOT the one I called) showed up, but when I asked the driver if his car was for me, he said "No"—he was waiting for someone else. We both waited and waited, but MY car never arrived and HIS passenger never showed up. Then I realized (DUHHHHH!) the car services mixed us up. The car that showed up earlier that picked up my neighbor was really the car service that I CALLED, and the car that waited for my neighbor was the one that SHE CALLED! Finally, I convinced the driver of this, and he finally took me in!

THAT's NOTHING TO SNEEZE AT!

I have a friend who's a germophobe. One day, in a restaurant, I had to blow my nose. I then put the tissue next to me, on the table, in case I had to sneeze again (why WASTE paper—even if it's just a tissue!). He then yelled out "RJ---put that AWAY! I don't want to SEE that!". When I told other friends about that, they said that the next time we're all at a restaurant, they will All deliberately start to blow their noses, just to ANNOY this, Guy!

THE "SHNORRER"

In Yiddish there's a word "Shnorrer", which means "taker" (rather than "giver"). It refers to a cheapskate---someone who wants everything for free). One night I and a group of friends met at a restaurant, and when it was time to leave, another friend (who arranged the venue) asked me to drive this woman (let's call her "Irene") home, since her car wasn't available. I reluctantly said "OK", even though it was late and I was tired and didn't really want to make the trip, which was out of my way. On the way to her house, she asked me to stop at a nearby fruit store---she said she just needed a few things and it would take only five minutes. I agreed. She wound up taking at least half an hour! Finally, she got back in my car and I drove her to her house. One of the reasons I was originally reluctant to drive her home (or drive ANYBODY home), was that my car looked like a PIG STY inside. That's because I use my car only for ME—I am not someone else's chauffeur! Anyway, my friend (who asked me to take her home in the first place) told me that after she got home, "Irene" called him up and told him that she'll NEVER ride in my car again, because the inside was FILTHY (which it WAS!). MY response to him was that next time she should take a CAB home! Did she think she was doing me a FAVOR by allowing me to drive her home????? She got a free ride! In addition, if she was so disturbed by the cleanliness of the inside of my car, why did she ask me to stop at the fruit store---would she really want to put bags of food in a filthy car???? I told my friend that next time, tell "Irene" not to do me any FAVORS! Let her call a CAB!

ACADEMY AWAAAAAAAAARRRRRRD!

When I was teaching in a NYC high school, I was on my break one day walking through the hall. I saw a group of 2 or 3 students wheeling the TV/VCR to their English class, but thought nothing of it, as it a common occurrence. The TV/VCR at that time was only available by reservation from the school library. Teachers, including myself, often show videos to their classes when there is a video available on the topic that they are teaching. It makes the topic more interesting (usually), and keeps the students' attention (usually---unless it is a boring topic). As I walked back through the hall, I saw the same group of students, laughing hysterically. "Mr. Nobleman, they shouted "you'll never guess what just happened! "What happened?" I said, inquisitively". "Out teacher, just set up a video of Macbeth, and he pressed the "play" button. Then he turned around and proceeded to walk to the back of the room. As he was walking, he heard the kids clapping and cheering---he couldn't figure out why"! When he turned around to see what all the cheering was about, he saw a couple performing a sex act! He immediately ran back to the VCR and shut it down!" They told me that he then sent monitors to bring the tape to the principal's office to report what happened" (and, I'm certain, to cover his own ass!) "Well…," I responded "I hope he (the teacher) at least gave out POPCORN!". I also, to this day, wonder whether the principal watched the tape himself, and whether he would have rated it "X", double X("XX"), or Triple X "XXX")!

WE'RE SEEING A MOVIE!!!?????"

Speaking of showing movies and videos to my classes, one day I was wheeling the TV/VCR through the hall to my class, pushing through the line in the hall to get to my classroom before the late bell rings. Some kid, who was also on his way to my class, saw me and yelled out, excitedly, "HEY, Mr. Nobleman, -----We're SEEING a MOVIE?????" "NO" I replied……, "I'm just wheeling the TV around!!!!!" "I'm just BORED"! From what I remember about the intelligence quotient of that particular kid, he probably thought I was serious! Maybe he figured that teachers get bored too, so they go around wheeling TV's around just for 'KICKS'!

"NOBLEMAN BUST HIS ASS!"

It was my first year of teaching—science teaching at a large city junior high school/middle school in Brooklyn. One winter day the streets were full of snow and ice. I was on my way to the school from the bus stop (I wasn't driving yet at the time). I was also running late, as was the usual for me. As I was crossing the street, which was full of ice, I fell down, backwards. Being younger, I was able to quickly pick myself up again and get to my class. I was hoping no students saw me fall, as it would be quite embarrassing! As soon as the kids entered the room, they shouted "HA-HA----Nobleman BUST his ASS!" About ten kids said the exact same phrase as they entered the room, one by one! (I guess some DID see me fall, after all!) I replied "Well, ---I hope I didn't make a POTHOLE in the street! (At the end of the day, in fact, I DID return to the scene to see if I DID INDEED make a pothole, but I didn't see any)!

FREE GUANO! (or) PIGEON-MAN OF BROOKLYN!

At the junior high/middle school I began teaching at, I came to class one morning before the kids arrived. I noticed that several desks had a white substance on them, but I didn't know immediately what it was. Then I realized it resembled bird feces that you often see on your car windshield. Then I noticed some window panels were missing, and I figured out that the previous night some birds must have entered the room through the missing window panels and 'did their business'! But, I didn't see any birds that were still there, so I figured that they had already 'checked-out'! Once the kids entered the room, they spotted a couple of pigeons perched on top of the light fixtures near the ceiling, and they began to yell and shout! We ran around the room, trying to chase the pigeons out, hoping they would fly out through the missing window panels, which was how they got in! But apparently they didn't remember HOW they got in, so they began to fly around the room, 'crapping' (defecating) all over the place at the same time! Finally, the assistant principal, hearing the RUCUS, came in the room and got a window pole and opened all the windows, and they finally flew out! What a way to start the day!

"PUT IT ON THE SCALE"!

I was visiting someone in the hospital, and went for lunch in the cafeteria, on my own. When I got there, it was basically self-serve. You picked what you wanted, put them on a large tray, then you went to the cashier to pay. I picked a salad which you put together yourself, and then you put it in a paper dish, with all the other food items, on a large tray. When I got to the cashier, she said to me "put it on the scale". So, I complied by putting the ENTIRE TRAY on the scale, as she told me to do! You should have seen the look of STUPIDITY she gave me, as she took the tray off the scale, then placed only the salad plate on it! I couldn't figure out why she looked at me that way----after all, I did exactly what she asked---I put it on the SCALE!

THE WAFFLE IRON FROM HELL!

I was upstate New York, staying at a hotel. This hotel gave complimentary breakfasts, as most hotels and motels do nowadays. But the breakfasts are basically self-serve. One of the items they offered were waffles, but you had to make them yourself---they provided the waffle batter, scoop-spoons/ladles, and an electric waffle iron, where you put the batter on, then close up both halves (top and bottom grills), then you turn it over and the waffles cook. When ready, a bell sounds, letting you know that the waffles are ready, at which point you turn the top and bottom parts right-side-up again, open the grills apart, and your VOILA! ---they are ready. BUT-----they don't tell you that there's a can of butter-spray that you must first put on the grills BEFORE you add the batter! So when I opened the two grill halves, the waffle material was all over the grills—and STUCK to them! So whoever came there after me would probably lose their waffle appetite!

GROUCHO DUCK!

I was visiting my aunt and uncle in West Palm Beach Florida, in a retirement community. One afternoon we sat by the swimming pool, sunning ourselves, with many other residents. I sat in the cot smoking my big cigar, as I watched the resident ducks walk around the pool. As I put the cigar between my fingers, (between puffs), one of the ducks came over and STOLE my cigar right out of my hand! He continued to walk around the pool with my cigar in his bill! I immediately yelled out "HEY---HE STOLE MY CIGAR!". Everyone was hysterical as we continued to watch the duck walk around with my cigar in his bill! After a few minutes, he dropped it, and I immediately ran over and retrieved it! I wiped off the duck saliva residue and continued to smoke it again. I guess 'Groucho Duck' didn't like the brand! Maybe it wasn't expensive or classy enough for him! Maybe he only liked HAVANA cigars! Sorry, Groucho—but beggars can't be choosers!

"DO YOU WANT TO FEEL THEM?"

I was on a subway train, where there weren't many passengers in the cars since the train had just left the origin station. Some woman in a tight blouse approaches me and says "My Nipples are hard---do you want to FEEL them?" I responded "Not right now, but thanks anyway---maybe some other time!" This will give you an idea of the many 'NUT JOBS' you meet in the subway!

COFFEE WARS

(1): Careful where you put the cup!

I went to a local electronics chain (now defunct), to buy a VCR. I brought the VCR up to the cashier, which apparently was manned by the store owner---the big boss! Apparently a few minutes before, he had sent one of the younger workers (named Mike) out to pick him up a cup of coffee, in a Styrofoam cup. He placed the cup on the cashier's check-out counter, but the cashier didn't see it because it was placed in the corner. When the cashier pulled my VCR towards him, the coffee cup spilled! "G-D DAMNNNNNN-IT MIKE!" he screamed—but he SCREAMED at the top of his lungs! The coffee spilled all over the counter! He screamed so loud that my ears were ringing! "OK—OK," said Mike. "I'll buy you another one---I'll buy you another one"! At the time I made believe I wasn't fazed at all by the situation. But I was HYSTERICAL all the way home! My ears are STILL ringing every time I think of that!

(2): COURTESY COFFEE MACIHNES THAT AREN'T SO COURTEOUS! (or) THE COFFEE MACHINE FROM HELL!

I went into a local bank to open up a savings account. The agents who were in charge of that up front were all busy, so they asked me have a seat and to wait about 10 minutes. They told me that in the meantime, I can go to the free coffee machine on the side and get a free coffee. When I went to the machine, it was like no other machine I've ever seen or used before. The coffee grinds were stored in small plastic cups—I think they're called "keurigs." As there were no instructions on how to use the machine, I figured I was supposed to open the keurig and pour the grinds out at below the pipe where the coffee comes out of. Instead, there were coffee grinds all over the machine! The agents had to come over and show me how the machine works---then they had to clean up the whole MESS that I made! I acted non-fazed, but again, I was HYSTERICAL all the way home!!!

THE DRIPPING WET UMBREELA!

I was on Jury duty a number of times, and this time it was Grand Jury. At the end of every case, the prosecutors would address the jury and discuss the idea of circumstantial evidence, explaining, as an example, that if it had been nice weather earlier that day, and suddenly someone enters the room with a "dripping wet umbrella", THAT is an example of circumstantial evidence for us to assume it's raining outside! The problem was that on Gand jury, we heard about 100 or more cases over a month's time, so we kept hearing about the "dripping wet umbrella" 100 or more times! One day I raised my hand and asked the prosecutor this question:" when you explain the idea to us about circumstantial evidence, could you POSSIBLY use another example, rather than the DRIPPING WET UMBRELLA?" She asked my "why"? I told her "last night I had a nightmare that I was walking down the street, minding my own business. SUDDENLY, I was being chased by a mob carrying a THOUSAND DRIPPING WET UMBRELLAS! She apologized, but said she HAD to continue to use that example as it was the court's standard example! (After THAT, I really DID have these nightmares---"THE DRIPPING WET UMBRELLAS FROM HELL"!

I DON'T KNOW!!!!!!!

I was driving to a local hospital one day to visit a family friend. I had been there many times in the past, but it was several miles from my home. As I was driving there, I decided to take what I thought was a shortcut. As the saying goes, "if it's not broken, don't' fix it!". I wound up getting lost! As I was driving through the streets, trying to find my way, I saw some guy coming out of his house. Based on the way he was walking, I should have realized he was having a bad day, but I asked him for directions to the hospital anyway. BIG MISTAKE! I called out to him "Excuse me, do you know the way to the (XXXXX) hospital? **"I DON'T KNOW**!!!" he SCREAMED at me!, as he kept on walking like he was passing through the gates of hell!

PICA-DILLY-DILLY!

I was a kid, about 9 years old, and my parents decided to send me to day camp (you can IMAGINE WHY!!!). Anyway, I had to walk to a local school, where a school bus picked us (other day campers) up. You know how kids can be mean, and make fun of each other. There was this one kid, a couple of years older and bigger than me, who the other kids liked to tease, because he kind of walked like a duck. They would often yell out to him (for unknown reasons) "Pica-Dilly-DILLY, and he would get mad, and often chase after them. What the heck "Pica-dilly-DILLY" actually meant, I didn't, (and still DON'T), know! After I saw that a few times, I did the SAME thing! Every time I saw him, I would yell "Pica-dilly-DILLY! Pica-dilly-DILLY! Pica-dilly-DILLY! and he would chase me! Luckily for me, he NEVER caught me, as I was a fast runner at that time (NOT anymore!). And, as you can guess, I HAD to be a fast runner then!

CRABAPPLES!!!

When I was a kid, about 7 years old, as you can guess, I was a HANDFUL!!! One day my parents took a ride to my aunt and uncle's house, about two hours away in Long Island. They had just built a swimming pool, the above-ground type that you can erect and take down in the summers and fall. They also had a crabapple tree nearby, which was LOADED with crabapples! I was thrilled watching the pool's electronic filter---the way the water moved through it, in and out, again and again, amazed me. Then I got an idea! What would happen if I threw some of the crabapples into the filter machine????? I found out that the machine would stop working, and my uncle would have to clean out the crabapples from it, then it would work again! This was a THRILL to me! So I kept doing it, and my uncle would have to come over and clean it out again... and again... and AGAIN! The first couple of times, my uncle must have thought the crabapples just fell of the tree on their own or by the wind, and into the pool., getting caught in the filter machine. But after a few more times, he realized that it was NO ACCIDENT—NO ACT OF NATURE! Finally, as he cleaned it out again (for about the FIFTH time), he realized that it was ME! He mumbled "G-D DAMN YOUUUUUUUU)!!!" My father heard him, and asked "What's'- a-matter JOE????" Then Uncle Joe answered, "NOTHING---just a little problem caused by the wind". I walked away very innocently----and decided that throwing crabapples into the pool wasn't such a good idea after ALL!

"LADIES AND GENTLEMEN……, LEND ME YOUR EARS"! ---- "OWWWWWWWWW!!!"

I was at a local pet shop which was selling all kinds of animals—birds, reptiles, amphibians, tropical fish, mice, rats, hamsters, gerbils, and even insects! The woman who owned the pet shop had a big white parrot as her personal pet, and she would walk around the store, showing off her parrot, often perched on her shoulder! When I approached the counter, ready to pay for something, she was at the cash register, with her playful parrot on her shoulder, playfully annoying her, jumping up and down, flapping its wings, moving up and down her arm, chirping all the while, but the owner didn't even seem to be the least bit fazed! Maybe the parrot was mad because the woman didn't acknowledge its presence, so, in an attempt to get acknowledged, BIT HER EARLOBE!

"OWWWWWWWWW!!!" she screamed. I made believe I didn't see ANYTHING! But I was HYSTERICAL all the way home!!!

FRIED FISH------------YOU PUT IT IN A DISH!

When I was in elementary school, in the fourth grade, there was a kid in the class who I became friendly with, named Marvin. What we had in common was that we liked to fool around and get into trouble (as you can probably imagine!). There was another teacher in the school whom we had class with just two or three times a week, named Mrs. Filish (the first "i" pronounced "eye"), for about an hour each time. For some UNKNOWN reason, Mrs. Filish did not care for me and Marvin too much. Marvin made up a name for her, "Mrs. Fried-Fish"! Every time we saw her, he would say "there's Mrs. Fried-Fish"! He said it in a very low voice so that only both of us heard it, and we would laugh! Then he actually made up a SONG about her: "Friiiiieeeed Fish—you put it in a DISH--it tastes so Fiiiiiiine---it's good with a bottle of wiiiiiiiiiine! Fried Fish---you PUT it in a DISH!" That was the whole song. Again, whenever we saw her, he would sing that song to me, again and again! And, of course, we would laugh! One day our class was going on a trip---I think it was to the Statue of Liberty. The class followed our regular teacher down the staircase, for several floors. Of course, Marvin and I always trailed behind, purposely, so we could horse around. That day, as me and Marvin were walking down the steps, well behind the rest of the class---GUESS who we ran into coming UP the steps-----none other than the FAMOUS Mrs. Filish! I and Marvin both said to her "Hy Mrs. Filish!" First I said it, then Marvin said it---to make her think we really liked her! She had NO IDEA how Marvin always 'DISSED HER'! After we thought she walked up the steps and was gone, Marvin yelled out "FRIIIIIIEEEEEED FISH! You PUT it in a DISH"! Then we both laughed! Unfortunately for us, Mrs. Filish hadn't quite reached the top of the staircase yet, and she HEARD him, but didn't quite understand what he said. So she summoned us both up the stairs, and asked me "WHAT did he CALL me?" I replied "I don't know---he always says stupid things, but I just let him talk and I don't even answer him!" Then Mrs. Filish warned Marvin that if he EVER calls her anything again, she would get him into trouble. Then we both went back down the stairs to catch up with our class. Our regular teacher then asked "What TOOK you two boys so long to get here?" I don't remember the excuse we gave, but I'm sure it was a lame excuse!

"ROAST PUFFIN AND WALRUS LIVER"!

About a decade ago I took a cruise to Iceland, Greenland, and northern Europe, leaving from Boston and returning to Boston, over about a four-week period. At every port, the ship provided shores excursions, and we had a large choice of them. In Iceland, we took a tour to a local fish and meat smoke-house, where they were to serve lunch as part of the tour package. But they did not tell us (a group of about 20 passengers) exactly what the dish would be. As we sat at the table waiting to be served, everyone was wondering what the dish would be. Let me tell you that on this tour, we saw much Iceland wildlife. We saw many---hundreds or thousands of beautiful colorful seabirds called puffins. They were EVERYWHERE. We also saw much sea life, like seals and whales, arctic fish, and possibly walruses. So as we sat at the table, again, everyone was wondering what the dish was going to be! Everyone was guessing and betting each other about it. So, in my WARPED sense of humor, but with a straight face, I yelled out "ROAST PUFFIN AND WALRUS LIVER"! You should have seen the look of DISBELIEF and DISGUST by most of the group, who probably BELIEVED me (and probably LOST their appetite)! (Actually, I think the meal was roast or fried chicken).

THE FISH THAT DIED!

I was on the subway one day, in the late afternoon, on a train during rush hour, when most people are returning home from work, and most are tired. Often, they fall asleep in their eats, if they are lucky enough to GET a seat! On this day, I had a seat and saw on old friend from the neighborhood, who then sat next to me. We were looking around and 'throwing the bull', when he suddenly pointed to a guy sitting opposite us. He said to me "take a look at the guy in the seat opposite us". I took a look and saw the guy sleeping, but his eyes were wide open and so was his mouth. "He then said "take a good LOOK at that guy, ---the FREAKIN' GUY looks like a FISH—that DIED"! Actually, he was RIGHT! The freakin' guy DID INDEED look like a FISH that died! Who knows—maybe he was a FISH in a past life! (Hopefully he was not a Piranha!).

THE 'ZHLUBBB' FACTOR!

When I was teaching high school in the NYC public schools, I was at a school where I and my supervisor, let's just say, didn't always quite see "eye to eye," to it put it mildly. I can't tell you my reasons for the way I felt about him, because that would be a book in itself (probably an entire VOLUME, at that)! Anyway, one day at a staff meeting, he literally and outwardly called me a "ZHLUB"! It didn't bother me because I would EXPECT that from him! Anyway, a few days later I was showing a colleague (who was present at that scene), some photos of my own chromosomes which I was able to prepare, as chromosome biology is my specialty. One of the chromosomes, for whatever reason, seemed to be missing a piece, so I showed my colleague the missing section and told him that I didn't know what it meant. He smiled and answered, "the ZHLUBBB Factor"!

2-2-LOO to TOO-TOO-LOO!

I was once on a cruise from Boston to Europe, and one of the cruise directors was originally from England. She likewise had a strong British accent. Every day, throughout the day, she would make announcements regarding the day's activities, information about ports of call, customs regulations, and many other matters. After every announcement, she would always sign off with "Too-Too-Loo!". After a while, we gave her the nickname "TOO-TOO-LOO"! One day, before the cruise ended, we heard that she left the ship, (reason unknown). So everybody began to say "TOO-TOO-LOO to TOO-TOO-LOO"!

RE-STOCKING THE SEWER!

When I was a kid, and even to this day, whenever I saw a lake, river, pond or any other body of water, I always walked over to it and stared inside, hoping to see fish or other living things (I guess that's why I'm a biologist today! But when I was a kid, and even to this day, even a SEWER piqued my interest! Sometimes looking down the sewer, I would see occasio0nal bubbles rise to the surface—most likely from living organisms like fish, possibly frogs, or bacteria! When I was about 8 years old, I thought there were FISH living down the sewer, and I often stood on the street corner with my fishing rod, fishing down the sewer (and although I NEVER caught anything, I remained undaunted!). People would often pass by, and ash "CATCH anything????" To re-stock the sewer, I used to go to a local fish market, bought things that were still living (clams, oysters, snails, crabs, mussels, scallops, even EELS!), and 'deposited' them down the sewer! So if you ever hear of any of those organisms that are found living down the NYC sewers---GUESS how they got there!

"MR. CLOTHES-PIN"!

When I was teaching high school, twice a year we held "open-school night", where parents are invited to come to the school to discuss the progress of their kids. Wanting to make a good impression, I asked my mother to dust off my sport jacket. This was not an easy job, because it had been YEARS since I ever SAW a sport jacket, let alone WEAR one, and it was probably stiff by now and full of dust (to say NOTHHING of the butterflies and moths, maybe even TERMITES that probably made a home of it! Anyway, she decided to air it out on the clothes-line for a day, to let the dust, butterflies, moths, and other inhabitants escape! So the parents' meetings went along well, --the meetings lasted about 3 hours, and I probably spoke to at least 25 parents. Another teacher shared the room with me, and she also spoke with many parents. When the meeting was finally over, both of us packed up and got ready to leave. As I was getting ready to leave, she asked me "Do you know you have a CLOTHES-PIN hanging down from the bottom of your sport jacket"? I said "WHAT clothes-pin?". Then I took off the sport jacket, examined it, and sure enough, there WAS a clothes-pin hanging down from it---I guess my mother forgot to take it off! "UH-OH!", I said, "I HOPE NO PARENTS SAW IT"! I didn't think they saw it because none of them said anything to me about it---so I was relieved! The next day, a girl in my class came up to me and said "MR. NOBLEMAN! MY MOTHER WAS HYSTERICAL ALL NIGHT" ---- Why were you wearing a CLOTHES -PIN on the back of your sport jacket"! I should have told her" Well, it's a new STYLE I'm trying to start"!

A QUESTION ABOUT THE SQUIRRELS!

When I was in my sophomore year of college, as a biology major, I was taking a field course called Field Studies in Zoology. We visited parks, zoos, museums, aquariums----anywhere there were animals that we could study, as well as plants and trees. One day we were at a park, and the professor stopped by a certain tree to lecture about it---I think it was either a horse chestnut tree or an Osage Orange tree. As she was lecturing, a straggler—a middle age man not part of the class nor the college, (and a little bit of a NUT JOB!) came by to listen. As he listened, he started making comments and adding material to the professor's lecture. Everybody was laughing, quietly or to themselves---because we wondered WHO this guy was and WHO invited him to stick his two cents in, which was NOBODY! As the professor continued her lecture about the tree, and while the students were gathered around her, the straggler continued to make comments and added his own material. After about ten minutes, when the professor was almost finished lecturing, he raised his hand and yelled out, "I got a question about the squirrels"! All the students at this point were hysterical! The professor then turned to him and said: "Thank you very much for your input! We appreciate it, but these are my students and they have work to do! So THANK YOU VERY MUCH! Thank you VERY much!" Then our group moved on to the next tree, and the straggler finally got the message that we didn't need his help anymore!

THE DISAPPEARING ACT!

When I was about 4 years old, I had relatives—an aunt and uncle and some cousins who lived around the corner from me. One day my mother and I went over to visit, and on their kitchen table I saw a small milk-chocolate bunny! My uncle was sitting at the table in front of the bunny, so I asked him if I could have it. He told me no, because he bought it specifically for his daughter (my younger cousin by about two years). So I figured out a way to get the chocolate bunny ANYWAY! When my mother came over to the table to talk to him, I asked her to pick me up and hold me. When he wasn't looking, I grabbed the chocolate bunny and ATE it, being careful not to let him see what I was doing! After the bunny was finished, I had my mother put me back down, and my uncle noticed the bunny had somehow disappeared. He looked around for it, then he asked me directly, "What happened to the chocolate bunny that I bought for Sheila (my younger cousin--- his daughter)"???? I looked at him, briefly and guilt fully and said, "I don't know". He just sat there and stared at me, at which time I ran quickly away into the next room!

THERE'S A FACE IN MY SOUP!

I often went to a local Chinese restaurant with a friend. The food was usually excellent, but some of the so-called customers were real WIERDOS! One day there was a guy eating alone at a table, who actually began to fall asleep over and over again during the meal. We could see he was definitely drunk. Sometimes while he was eating his soup, his face almost fell right into the bowl! Finally, the waiter came over and told him "Sir---this is a RESTAURANT—you cannot SLEEP here! The guy responded in a drunken tone "Your SOUP made me SICK!", blaming it on the SOUP! Again, the waiter told him---"You cannot SLEEP here!" Eventually, the guy decided it was time to leave, and the waiter gave him the bill. Apparently, the guy had no money to pay the bill---he said he couldn't find his wallet, so he told the waiter that he could not pay the bill because he left his wallet home, and besides that, their SOUP made him SICK! He told the waiter that he would bring him the money next week, when he gets paid. The waiter told him he must pay the bill NOW, or he'll have to call the police. The guy answered by saying he would call his wife, who would bring the money over because he didn't live very far. The waiter gave him the telephone (there were no cell phones then), and the guy dialed his home. When his wife answered, the guy told her, in a very drunken tone that he was in the restaurant and needed cash to pay his bill. All of a sudden, we heard "CLANK!"! Obviously is wife was sick and tired of his drunken lifestyle---so obviously she was not about to come to his rescue! Now he had a PROBLEM---no money to pay the bill! Again, the waiter told him that if he doesn't pay NOW, they will be forced to call the POLICE! Again, the guy asked him to hold off until next week when he gets paid and he would return to pay it! Next thing we knew, the waiter, who was also the cashier, called the police. They came in a few minutes, saw that the guy was drunk, and realized that he could not pay the bill, and asked the waiter if he wanted to press charges so they could arrest him. The waiter declined to have the bum arrested, but he told him never to come there again, and the bum left! We figured the incident would just be forgotten, and it seemed like it was, because for the next couple of weeks, when I and my friend ate there, we neither saw nor heard anything more about the incident.

About two weeks later I returned to the restaurant to order take-out, and asked the same waiter if the guy ever came back to pay his bill. The waiter told me no, and that he hadn't seen the guy since. Five minutes later, as I was waiting for my take-out order, GUESS who walks in----that SAME guy (SOBER this time!) with a friend. They asked to be seated, but the waiter refused, telling them that they was not welcome there because the guy didn't pay his bill last time! What I found AMAZING was that the guy hadn't returned since the incident, until FIVE MINUTES after I asked the waiter if he ever saw the guy again! To this day, I wonder if that was just a COINCIDENCE, or if 'other forces' were at play!

THE MYSTERY OF THE GARNISHED CIGARETTE!

In the same restaurant I mentioned earlier (see "There's a FACE in my Soup!)", I and my friend were eating, and there was a young woman, probably in her 20's, sitting alone at the table in front of us. After about ten minutes, she yells out, at the top of her voice "OHHH! ---I CAN'T EAT THIS!" She calls the waitress over and shows her that there was a CIGARETTE in her chow-mein! She tried to tell the waitress that she couldn't finish the meal because whomever cooked it either deliberately threw or accidently dropped a CIGARETTE in the food, and showed the waitress the cigarette in the dish!! What we couldn't figure out was HOW she could eat almost the ENTIRE the meal and not notice the cigarette until she was almost finished eating! Obviously, she just didn't want to PAY for it, so she threw one of her OWN cigarettes into the dish, right in the center, as an excuse for not paying! Like I saw previously, the food in that restaurant was excellent, but some of the customers who ate there were real WIERDOS!

GIVE IT TO THE CAT!

In the same restaurant I described above, one day I and my friend were eating there, but I couldn't finish my main dish—I was too stuffed. My friend was somewhat of a 'glutton', and he could probably eat 24/7, non-stop! So when I couldn't finish my main dish, he asked me if I was going to get a 'doggie bag' and take it home, but being stuffed and lazy, I told him no. So he asked if HE could have it (for RIGHT THEN, not for home). I told him it was OK with me, so I put it into is dish using my fork, and he began to DEVOUR it (with a PASSION!). I then yelled out---"Yeah—give it to the CAT! Give it to the CAT!" The other customers were HYSTERICAL!

HOW I INVENTED THE "SELFIE"!

A few decades ago, I joined a record club where they sent me about 7 or 8 vinyl albums (there were no CDs then), and one of the albums was by a rock group from the 60's. One of the female group members was so beautiful that I immediately fell in love with her, so I decided to send her a fan letter. She actually answered me by sending a sheet of her photos, and on it she wrote "To RJ with very best wises!", and underneath she signed her name! EXCITED, I decided to send her a photo of myself as well, but I didn't want to ask anyone to snap the photo, because they might ask me why I needed it (and I didn't want to tell them!). So I took my camera, put in film, then pointed the camera, backwards at my face (while I was smoking my cigar!), and snapped my picture. Then had it developed and sent it to her! So I believe this was actually the first "selfie", and if true, that would mean that I actually invented the first "selfie"! I even sent her some photos my basset hound, "Axelrod"! I continued to write to her, but never received any more responses (I wonder WHY!). She probably thought (knew?) that I was some kind of NUT! (and, in retrospect, I guess she was RIGHT!).

BE CAREFUL WHAT YOU WEAR!

I had an aunt and uncle who lived most of their life right here in Brooklyn, only about a mile from my house. Years later, they retired and moved to a few different places, mainly in Massachusetts, in the Cape Cod region. After my uncle passed away, the family held a memorial service, up in the Cape Cod region, where they lived. So I went to the service, and stayed the first night in a motel. But in the morning I went first to a local tavern for breakfast. I didn't realize it when I was dressing, but I was wearing a shirt that read "YANKEE STADIUM", with a picture of the stadium on it---and at the tavern I realized that it was NOT the smartest thing to do! So I put a bib over my head, neck, and chest, finished my meal, and GOT THE HELL OUT OF THERE as soon as possible! LUCKY ME!

"MY GRANDMOTHER DID IT!"

When I was about six years old, my parents rented a bungalow for the summer, upstate New York. I was always hanging around the laundry room, there, because I had an obsession for washing machines! One day my grandmother came by to use the machines, and somehow she screwed it up, so the machines stopped working. The owner came by to try to fix it up, but he had a difficult time, and he kept mumbling things under ns breath, wondering WHO screwed up the machines! As I was always taught not to tell a lie, I yelled out "MY GRANDMOTHER DID IT!!". I guess the old phrase "children should be seen and not heard" was true! My mother (her daughter) told me that she never heard the end of that"!

"WELL...THEY GOTTA EAT TOO!"

When I was teaching biology at a NYC high school, the science department had a "prep room", where materials for demonstrations and lab experiments were prepared and stored. The person in charge of the prep room was called a "laboratory specialist. He or she was in charge of preparing the materials and keeping the room in order. We began to get infested with mice, and one of the teachers began complaining to the laboratory specialist that he (the lab specialist) should be cleaning up all the closets, drawers, and cabinets from food crumbs so that mice would stay out of them and hopefully out of the prep room! The laboratory specialist was annoyed that the teacher was 'invading his turf ', by telling him how to do his job, and he answered "Well, THEY (the mice) GOTTA EAT TOO!"!

"OH! WHAT A TANGLED WEB (FISHING LINE) WE WEAVE!"

I'm not sure where that quote came from, but I think it was from Shakespeare? Anyway, when I was about ten years old, the family vacationed at a hotel in the Catskills---in Swan Lake, NY. The hotel was up on a steep hill, and there was a lake below with a small bridge where many people went fishing. Rather than staying with the hotel day camp, I spent most of my days on the bridge, watching people fish. One day an elderly man came there to fish, but his fishing line was all tangled up on his rod! I passed by him and saw him trying to untangle the mess, but I realized this was not going to be a fast job! When I saw how tangled the rod was, I began cracking up—HYSTERICALLY! An hour later, this guy was standing there, still trying to untangle the line from his rod! An hour later, it was the same story! He must have spent about five hours trying to untangle the line from his rod, and every time I passed by, I laughed harder and harder! I don't think he ever untangled the line off his rod, which he WASTED the whole day trying to do!

A REAL 'DENNIS THE MENACE'! ---or---
THE RETURN OF THE PEST!

On the other side of the bridge, there was a man who came to fish every day, but he was not the most 'friendly' individual. He was not 'social' by any means, and did not like to talk much, especially to ten-year-old pestering kids (like me!). One day he caught a bullhead catfish, and he put it in a bucket with water. I kept asking him all kinds of annoying questions, like what he was going to do with the catfish, if he was going to cook and eat it. He told me he would, but if he didn't like the taste, he had cats at home that would eat it. Getting him to answer my annoying questions was like 'pulling teeth'! Anyway, the next day I passed by, to watch him fish again, and the first thing he said to me was "Are YOU here again!!!! To PESTER again!!!!

ROLLER DERBY! ---or---
BECOMING THE CHAIR-MAN!

Just a few years ago I was taking a college physics class, and the chairs in the room were a real HAZARD! They had wheels on the bottom, and when you tried to get up out of the chairs, they rolled backward! In addition, when you got out of them, besides rolling backward, they often tumbled over, so you had to get out of them very slowly and carefully! When the class was over, I forgot about their hazardous quality---I first rolled about five feet backward, then I fell off the chair backward, along with the entire chair! Upon seeing this, the professor told me to be careful, because the day before that, the same thing happened to HIM! When I fell over, I'm surprised I didn't cause an EARTHQUAKE!

THE HORSE THAT "DON'T LOOK TOO GOOD TODAY"!

The following story was not one that I witnessed myself, but was told to me by a relative, and I'm certain it actually occurred, although it was several decades ago.

It seems that, at that time, there was a horse stable in Prospect Park, a tree-rich park right here in Brooklyn, (trees DO grow in Brooklyn, even to this day)! People would often 'rent' horses, if they were experienced riders, to get their kicks by riding the horse around. Potential riders would look over the horses that were available, and then they would choose the horse they wanted to ride. The owner of the stable was from another country—probably from eastern Europe, and his English wasn't exactly up to par. One day a medical doctor came into the stable to choose a horse to ride. He looked around several times, then he picked a horse. When he told the stable owner which horse he wanted, the owner balked. He told the doctor not to pick that horse, because, he said, "he doesn't look too good today!". The doctor re-examined the horse, and said "looks good to MEEEEE"! And he insisted he wanted THAT horse, so the stable owner complied and let him ride that horse. After riding for a few minutes, the horse crashed into a tree! It turns out that the horse was BLIND! When the stable owner told the doctor "he don't look too good today", what he really meant was that the horse wasn't SEEING too well that day! Goes to show ya'---don't mess with the KING'S ENGLISH!

"OH-SHIT!!! OH-SHIT!!! NOBLEMAN'S TALKING TO A PIECE OF CHALK!!!"

I was teaching high school, and my father had recently passed away at the age of 97. The main way I was able to deal with that was to visit spirit mediums, which I learned about watching the show "Unsolved Mysteries". Many or most people do not believe in mediums, but I can tell you, the first medium I went to in Pennsylvania was really on the ball! She told me things about my father that she could not have POSSIBLY known, nor could she have ever found that information on the internet! Anyway, one of the things she told me was that my father was going to send me pennies, and other coins, to let me know that he is still with me in spirit form. After that session, I was finding pennies and all sorts of other coins on the ground and other places all over the place! She also told me that when I find these coins, I should say a little prayer or a phrase of thanks! So every time I found a coin, no matter where it was, I picked it up and spoke to it, expressing my gratitude!

One day at the high school, the bell rang ending the current period, and on the floor below the blackboard were pieces of chalk that had fallen, but there was also a coin. So I picked up the coin, and, as usual, began talking to it, expressing my gratitude. Students were passing through the hall at that time, and I had my classroom door open. Some kid passed by and saw me talking to the coin, but he thought it was a piece of chalk I was talking to! All of a sudden, he screams out "OH SHIT!!! OH-SHIT!!! Nobleman's talking to a piece of CHALK!!!" I just collected my books and went to my next class!

"SHUT-UUUUUUPPPPPPPPPPPP!"

I was a passenger in a car one day, and we were stopped at a red light. As we were waiting for the (long) red light to change, I saw some teenager on the street calling up to his girlfriend's apartment, by her window. Apparently, he wanted her to come and hang out, or maybe he just wanted to talk to her. She didn't come out, nor come to the window, but the girl's mother came to the window, and apparently, she didn't want him to talk to her daughter, or maybe she didn't even want him to be her daughter's boyfriend. She told him that her daughter was not coming out, and she didn't want her to even talk to him! The teen and the girl's mother began to argue, and then he yelled to her "SHUT-UP!" The mother was PISSED, and told him "DON'T TELL ME TO SHUT-UP! DON'T YOU **EVER** TELL ME TO SHUT-UP!!! The teen, obviously PISSED-OFF, then SCREAMED at her "SHUT-UUUUPPPPPPPPPPPPP!!!!" Finally, the girl's father came to the window, and you could see he was getting ready to 'convince' the teen that he was not happy that he told his wife (the girl's mother) to SHUT-UP! You could see him immediately leave the window to come out to confront the teen! Since I was a passenger in the car, we drove away after the red light changed. So how did the story end????? Your guess is as good as mine!

GOOD, BUT A BIT TOO 'PEPPERY'!

I went to a very well known local pizza place and ordered a couple of slices. There was an open window where you were served, after which, if it were a nice day, people ate their pizza outside at tables. There was another table where people could add condiments to their slices---salt, black pepper, the red hot pepper flakes, garlic, etc., but this was NOT done at the open window, which was used just to serve the food. Someone somehow left the black pepper shaker at the serving window, so, as someone who likes pepper, I began sprinkling the pepper by the serving window. All of a sudden, I see the server making faces, closing is nose and mouth and eyes, and motioning with his hands for me to stop adding the pepper to the pizza. I couldn't figure out why! What happened was that there was a wind which was blowing the pepper into the server's face—his nose, eyes, and mouth! "OH, OH, SORRY", I said! Then I took my pizza slices and walked to the bench, very innocently!

THE SQUIRRELS ARE COMING!
THE SQUIRRELS ARE COMING!

I was at an amusement park in rural Pennsylvania. It was a hot day, and after a while I decided to sit in an open, grassy area to rest and take it easy. After a half-an hour or so, all of a sudden, I see two squirrels running very fast! One was chasing the other! Whether they were fighting or playing I don't know, but I don't think they saw me sitting there, and the squirrels were COMING DIRECTLY AT ME! I knew a collision was eminent, so I bent over and put my hands over my head and face---to take cover! At the last second, they managed to miss me by a fraction of an inch! A girl sitting near me saw the whole event unfold, and laughed out loud, HYSTERICALLY! Next time I'll put a sign there---"TO THE SQUIRRELS---WALK, DON'T RUN!"

WILD GOOSE CHASE!

I was visiting another country for a couple of weeks— (I won't tell you what country it was—let it be nameless!) I also am fluent in their language, although I can't speak it like a native, but I can easily get by. Anyway, a number of times while I was there, I needed to visit a certain building or company, but I didn't know where it was actually located, and I was a pedestrian. What I would do was to go to the approximate location, and ask passers-by for directions. All I can tell you is that here in Brooklyn, if someone asked me for directions to a location, if I knew where it was, I would gladly tell them so, and I would give them the best possible directions. If I didn't know the location, I would simply tell the person that I was sorry, but I don't know the location, and advise them to ask others. So in the country I was in, when I asked a passer-by the directions to a specific location, they might tell me "it's two blocks straight ahead, then, turn right at the corner, and then walk another three blocks." When I did that, I still couldn't find the building, so I would ask another passer-by for directions. They might then tell me "turn left at the corner, then walk two blocks straight, then turn right, and walk another three blocks straight!" This went on over and over again; I don't know HOW many blocks I walked—sometimes I would wind up at the SAME place where I asked the first passer-by. I don't know WHY they did this—maybe they were just too embarrassed to tell me that they did not know the location; maybe they were just too STUPID to realize they just didn't know, or maybe for some oddball reason they did it PURPOSELY! WHO KNOWS!!! The bright side is that at least I got to exercise my legs!

HOW I DEAL WITH 'NUISANCE' CALLS: TELEMARKETERS, ROBO-CALLERS, AND SCAMMERS!

Most of us, I believe, are sick and tired of all those nuisance phone calls, trying to sell you this or that, telling you you've won millions in some contest you know you never entered, or telling you that your grandson was arrested in some town you never heard of, and needs money immediately to bail him out! Most of us know a scam when we hear one, but the callers are hoping you are one of the few who are so GULLIBLE that you actually BELIEVE what you're hearing!

My technique of dealing with such calls is to "play along" with the script! For example, if I get a call from a number I don't recognize, then as soon as I answer, I'll say "HHELLO! HOW 'YA DOIN'! WHAT ARE YOU SELLING TODAY?" The response I almost always get is a chuckle---"I'm NOT SELLING ANYTHING!", then you find out that indeed, they are trying to sell you something! The only problem with that is that the call may actually be important! One caller told me that my car had been stolen and was found abandoned in Texas. Then they told me that BLOOD was found in the car! MY response to them was "if blood was found in the car, why didn't you put a BAND-AID on it?"!! Some callers tell me, often, that I won several million dollars in a sweepstakes that I knew I never even entered, or a sweepstakes that I DID enter but the odds of winning a big prize were 6 billion to one! My response to them is "OK, just send me the freakin' money, but try NOT to send it in PENNIES or NICKELS"! Another caller may tell me that my grandson Michael was in a car accident in a state all the way across the country, and that his wife, who is pregnant, was with him in the car. (I don't have a grandson named Michael, nor do I even HAVE a grandson)! So my response is to tell "Michael" that I will be wiring him money in a hour from now, and to WAIT at the money exchange office until it arrives! Sometimes the person calling would HIMSELF claim to be my grandson Michael (which I do not have!), and I would play along by saying "OH! MICHAEL! LONG TIME NO SEE! I HAVEN'T HEARD FROM YOU IN SOOOOOO LONG! HOW ARE YA' DOING??? HOW'S YOUR WIFE AND THE KIDS?"! After a short time, the scammers realize that it is ME who is SCAMMING THEM—and they hang up!

BOOOOOOOOOM!

I was walking down the avenue in my neighborhood one afternoon, and was walking into a store. There was a delivery truck double-parked across the street, making a delivery, and the driver was out of the truck, delivering the goods to whomever. All of a sudden, the people hear a big SIREN---it was a FIRE ENGINE en route to a fire somewhere. As the fire engine turned somewhat to pass the double-parked delivery truck, I guess it got a little too close. The tires on that fire engine were HUMONGOUS! All of a sudden, as the fire engine passes, we hear this giant "BOOOOOOOOOM"! Nobody knew what the sound was at first, but it sounded like a giant CANNON! It turned out that as the fire engine tried to pass the double-parked delivery truck, it scraped its front fender, shearing part of it off. The cut, sharp hunk of fender scraped against the delivery truck, BURSTING the fire engine's TIRE! I guess you might call it a "SONIC BOOM"! It was just like a CANNON, but no MAN was shot out of it! Hopefully the driver of the delivery truck might think twice the next time he decides to double-park--- (but probably not)!

THE FORTUNE COOKIE FROM HELL!

I and a few friends got together one night for dinner at a local Chinese restaurant. Like all Chinese restaurants, at the end of the meal they give you one or more fortune cookies. In general, these cookies predict good fortunes--- great things that will befall you—good tidings. Sometimes, instead of actual fortunes, or combined with a good fortune, they give you words of wisdom, usually old Chinese proverbs, usually originating with the words of Confucius! For example, a fortune cookie I received today reads "Your smile brings happiness to everyone you meet!". I had NEVER YET seen any NEGATIVE fortune---no evil tidings, at least until that night!

Earlier that day one of the women friends received bad news. Her nephew was just diagnosed with a form of cancer---I believe it was some type of lymphoma. The good news was that the doctors told her that type of cancer was usually treatable and curable, if caught in the early stages and if the victim was strong and healthy enough to withstand radiation and chemotherapy. Her nephew fit this description. He was energetic and only eighteen years old. Doctors were convinced that with treatment, he would be cured!

As I said, I had NEVER seen a fortune cookie that was evil or negative before. On that night, after the meal, we all opened our fortune cookie. All of use received good, positive fortunes, but when the woman in question opened HER fortune cookie, the fortune read "YOUR TROUBLES ARE JUST BEGINNING"! That was the FIRST, and so far the ONLY time, I had ever seen a fortune cookie with a NEGATIVE prediction! I didn't even THINK NEGATIVE fortune cookies were ever even printed! She was SHOCKED! Luckily, within a few months, her nephew was indeed cured! But the receipt of a NEGATIVE fortune was indeed STRANGE!

"UH-UH-UH-UH-UH-UH-UH-UH-UH-UH-UH-UH-UH-UH-UH-UH-UH"!!!

This story was told to me by a close friend, and even though I didn't witness it myself, I'm CERTAIN it is true!

It seems that in my friend's neighborhood, there was a group of about 5 friends, all teen boys... At night, they used to sit on one kid's (call him "Jeff") front stoop, and for a couple hours they would just horse around and 'throw the bull'! Sometimes the guy's parents would come out for a while and join the 'bull session'! One day the teen who lived at the house went for a vacation, I think to somewhere out west. Early that evening, his parents drove him to the airport to see him off, but his flight was not scheduled to leave for a couple more hours, so they bid him farewell and wished him a safe and enjoyable trip! Later that evening, about the time his plane was set to take off, his friends and his parents again gathered on front of their stoop for the typical 'throw the bull' session, even in his temporary absence. As they were conversing, a plane could be seen and heard from above. They all looked up, and one of his parents said "OH!!! I bet that's JEFF'S plane right now!" One of the 'friends", (and I use that term loosely!) probably another 'genius' looked up at the plane, and said "OH YEAH?"! That's JEFF'S plane?", then, making believe he had a high-powered MACHINE GUN, he pointed the imaginary gun upward at the plane, and said, imitating the sound of a machine gun, "UH-UH-UH-UH-UH-UH-UH-UH-UH-UH-UH-UH-UH-UH-UH-UH!!!", making believe he was trying to SHOOT the plane down! Are parents just LOOKED at him, in SHOCK! With "friends" like THAT, WHO needs ENEMIES?!!!

"YOU MADE ME LOSE MY FLY????---- WHAMMMMMMM!!!"

I and my parents were vacationing one summer, decades ago, at a farm and resort upstate New York. I was about 13 years old, and my maternal grandparents went there with us. We were all sitting in wooden chairs one day, just relaxing, with a group of other guests when we noticed some kid, about 5 years old, sitting in the chair next to my grandmother, fiddling around with something. Apparently, he found a dead fly in the grass, and he was examining it (he probably was a future entomologist!). We thought nothing of it, figuring he was just a kid, and "boys will be boys"! My grandmother, about 85 years old, was sitting in the chair right next to him, but had no idea what he was looking at or what he was doing (nor did she care!). People asked him what he was doing, and he said that he was playing with a dead fly he found in the grass below. You could clearly see he was really 'into' the dead fly! My grandmother still had no idea what he was playing with. Then he held the fly up and showed it to everybody, then he showed it in better detail, to my grandmother. Seeing the dead fly, she got scared and yelled "WOOOOOO" ---GET THAT OUT OF HERE!", and with that she pushed the kid's hands away! This caused the fly to fall out of his hands, and into the grass below. He immediately searched through the grass for a few minutes, but all in vain! No fly could be found! Then, ENFURIATED, he yelled to my grandmother "You made me LOSE my FLY? then "WHAM", he punched my grandmother in the arm! Then he went crying back to his mother, because he lost his fly!

THE OBSCENE PHONE CALL THAT WASN'T!

My aunt Pearl was my favorite aunt, and my favorite relative at that! When I was a teen, I had 'friends' that I often got into trouble with ("Boys will be Boys"!) Sometimes we would make crank phone calls to each other's' homes. Sometimes we would order pizzas to be delivered to each other's' homes that were not legitimate! One of us once ordered 36 buckets of fried chicken to be delivered, but luckily, the store owner was suspicious and called the family to verify the order first! Of course, none of us would ever ADMIT that we did these things, so we never knew for sure WHO did WHAT!

One day, I was home alone, and the telephone rang---there was no such thing as caller ID in those days. As soon as I picked up and said "hello", the voice on the other end said, (like an owl) "HOOOOOOOOOOOOOOOO"! HOOOOOOOOOOOOOOOO"! "HOOOOOOOOOOOOOOO"! Again I asked "who IS this", and again I heard "HOOOOOOOOOOOO!" "HOOOOOOOOOOOO!", "HOOOOOOOOOOOOOOOOOOO!"! This went on about two or three more times, and then I realized it must be one of my so-called "friends" making a CRANK call! So I got PISSED, and finally I yelled back "F-YOU"! (But I actually said the entire words!). As soon as I said that, the voice on the other end yelled back, in SHOCK "WHHHHHAT"! "WHHHHHHAT"! "WHHHHHHHHHHHAT!" The female voice couldn't believe that her 'goody-goody-two-shoes' nephew would SAY that! (Or that I even KNEW such words!). It turned out that it wasn't a crank call at all, it was my aunt Pearl just playing around! After THAT, she never played around anymore when she called!

THE SNOWSTORM IN MAY!

Here in Brooklyn, we rarely get snowstorms in April, and I've NEVER SEEN as snowstorm here in May, but one morning in mid may I opened my front door to see what I thought was about three inches of snow on the ground! I couldn't believe it. When I went outside to examine it, I realized it was NOT SNOW at all! It was pieces of white styrofoam, the type used in packing! What had happened was that a business opened up across the street, which often received deliveries of large packages and crates. Apparently, one of the crates fell off the delivery truck and broke open, and the styrofoam pieces went all over the street and sidewalks! You would THINK those S.O.B.'s that delivered the crate would have swept it up, or at least would have TRIED to sweep up as much as possible, but they didn't! The just delivered the broken crate and left! Just to be sure I would not get ticketed by the sanitation department, I came out with a broom and swept away the 'snow" (by sweeping it onto my NEIGHBOR'S property)!!!

LOOK OUT BELOOOOOOOOOOOOOW!

My first basset hound was a nice dog, but relatively lazy! Every day, we would let her outside into our back yard several times to romp around, take a sun bath, and do her business. In order to get into the back yard, though, she would have to first go on the back porch (made of planks of wood), and then walk down (only) about 5 steps. But she was usually too lazy to do so. Often, if not MOST of the time, she would do her business right on the back porch itself, rather than walk down those few steps into the yard. Whenever she urinated on the porch itself, the urine would spill down the narrow space between the wooden planks to the concrete below. One day my father, who was a gardener and landscaper by trade, was underneath the back porch, cementing cracks in the concrete below. I guess he didn't realize that the DOG was on the porch, lying down and taking a sunbath (which she LOVED to do!). Apparently, a few minutes later, she had to urinate, and my father suddenly noticed and heard a 'waterfall' nearby! The 'waterfall' missed his head by only a few inches! After that time, whenever he went under the porch to do any work, he always LOOKED on the TOP first, to be sure the 'sunbather' wasn't already there FIRST!

CANE AND ABLE! -or- WHEN IT COMES TO USING A CANE, AM I ABLE????

When I was a kid, again, as I think I may have mentioned before, I was basically a "Dennis the Menace"! When I was about 5 or 6 years old, there was an old man who lived across the street, who walked with a cane. To me, walking with a cane looked like FUN! And I guess I was a bit jealous that HE had a cane but I did not, so, one day while he was walking down the street with his cane, I walked over to him and first shook his hand----THEN, I STOLE his cane and began happily and proudly walking down the block with it! I was so happy I finally got to walk with a cane! The old man just STOOD there, motionless, as he needed the cane to get around! My older cousin, who saw the whole thing unfold, made me give the man his cane back! She was hysterical over the matter, and even the old man smiled when he got his cane back! The ironic/'karmic' thing is that today, due to a foot problem I developed a few tears ago, I NOW HAVE TO WALK WITH A CANE TOO!

TWO LEFT FEET!

A number of years ago my friend Jerry got married. Whenever we had previously gone to parties, his mother always asked me to dance with her, but I refused because I am NOT a dancer! But at his wedding, when she asked me to dance with her, how could I refuse? So I agreed, reluctantly, to dance with her. I don't know HOW MANY TIMES I stepped on her feet! Interestingly, after that, I don't remember her ever asking me to dance with her again!

PICTURE PERFECT!

When I was about 10 years old, I had some relatives that lived only a few blocks away. My uncle was heavily into photography, although he was not a professional photographer, he really knew his photography, and he had many different cameras with a variety of magnifying lenses. One day the extended family met at his home to take a family photograph--- probably there were about 20 people present, and we all lined up for the photo session. The adults were standing in a group based on height, and the kids, I amongst them, were seated in the front. When he said "SAY CHEESE", I made a funny, outrageous STUPID FACE! (I was known for making stupid faces in those days, as well as for sticking my tongue out at people!). When the large, probably 10 X 20 black and white photo was developed, you could see the 20 or so relatives, all smiling, but I was in the corner of the first row, making a really STUPID face! Basically, I RUINED the entire photo! One day, 20 or more years later, I and my mother were looking through old papers, and we found the photo! We were looking at the STUPID face I made when the picture was snapped, and I asked my mother what the other relatives said about it. "NOTHING!", she said--- "they were EXPECTING that from you"!

SOMETIMES, IT PAYS TO PROCRASTINATE!

In 1998 I bought my first car, but I never really serviced it enough. When things began to go wrong, if it was not an emergency and the car was still running, I didn't bother to get it fixed. I don't remember ever even taking it to a car wash! Eventually the rear windows did not close completely, and when closed, or nearly completely closed, they were not locked in place. All one had to do was to push the windows downward with their hands, and they would open completely! People kept asking me WHEN I would be going to get the car fixed up!

One day I went to visit a friend's home, and parked the car a couple of blocks away. When I arrived, I realized that my keys (car keys and house keys all attached to one ring), were missing. "UH OH!", I thought to myself, now not only won't I be able to get into and start my car, but I won't be able to get into my HOUSE either! Worrying that I might have to call and wait for AAA, I immediately went back to my car, and was able to push down the back windows! I then managed to open the door and get back in and retrieve my keys! This was all because I procrastinated getting the back windows fixed! Had I previously had them fixed, I'd never be able to retrieve my keys (CAR keys and HOUSE keys!) without professional help! Sometimes it PAYS to procrastinate!

IN THE WINE-MAKING (OR 'GLASS-BLOWING') BUSINESS!

When I was a young teen, about 13, we had a crabapple tree growing in our front yard. The apples were many—probably hundreds, but they were MAAAAAAAAD SOUR! I felt it was a waste to throw them away, or just let them fall and rot, so I had a great idea! I would make crabapple WINE out of them. I put a bunch of them in a glass bottle, added some water and sugar, and yeast, and TIGHTLY closed the cap, then I waited for a few days for wine to form. The problem was that at that time I did not understand the fermentation process (I was not officially a 'biologist' yet). I did not understand that the process produces carbon dioxide GAS while it produces alcohol. I also didn't understand the laws of physics, that as a gas builds up in a closed container, whether plastic or glass, if it cannot escape, eventually the container will build up PRESSURE, then pop open or EXPLODE! So after a few days of fermentation, the gas built up, and the entire bottle EXPLODED!!! When I went down the basement to see what happened, there was glass 'wine', liquid, and mashed up CRABAPPLES all over the floor! The blast was so powerful that shards of glass were found in the adjacent basement room about 20 feet away! It's a good thing nobody was down there at the time of the event! That being said, I still never quite understood why my parents were so reluctant to leave me HOME ALONE!

NO MICROSCOPES TODAY!

One of the things I admire professional comedians for the most is their ability to come up with one-liners spontaneously and quickly! Such was the case for me, one day when I was teaching my high school biology class. I asked the class a question (I don't remember what it was), and all of a sudden, some kid (who was rather smart and never caused me any problems before) answered "MY D---!" (his male organ!). I was shocked that a relatively smart kid, who was never a 'problem' before, would say that. (Maybe he was just having a bad day). My IMMEDIATE response was "NO!-NO!-NO!-NO!-NO! We're not using MICROSCOPES today!" Out of a class of about 25 students, only one kid, a relatively smart girl, began laughing, HYSTERICALLY! Obviously, she was the only one who got the joke! Even the kid who made the wise-crack was silent---I don't think even HE got the joke EITHER! I then said to the hysterical girl, "THAT was GOOD, right?" In between laughs, she responded "YEAAAAAAAAAAAH!"! Yet, even several minutes later, none of the others got the joke! (I hope whomever is reading this story now can 'get it')! And I'm PROUD of myself for being able to come with the one-liner so fast!

I DID THAT PURPOSELY!!!!!

Besides teaching high school for 30 years, I also taught at various local NYC colleges and community/two-year colleges after I received my Ph.D. in biology on an adjunct (part-time) basis. Since I had to travel there by subway, I was always always a bit late, usually no more than 10 minutes or less, but sometimes even more! So on the first class meeting, I tried to get there extra early, and I told the students of my transportation problem, and that if I am late, I'm definitely on my way over, and that they should just take their seats and wait for me to arrive. I had a weekend class that met on Sundays, starting at 8 AM. Due to the early time and the NYC subways, on the second session I was late—this time by about 15 minutes, and being only the second class meeting, I could not remember most of the names and faces in my class, nor even the EXACT room number! So on that day, being 15 minutes late, I has HOPED the students would remember that I am on my way over, and to wait for me to arrive! When I arrived at about 8:20 AM, I ran as fast as possible to the class, hoping they had not as yet left! I passed by the first open room I saw, and saw a class full of students, and ASSUMED (as Felix Unger would say, "NEVER ASS-U-ME"!) I thanked the class for waiting, and immediately began lecturing on today's topic. After lecturing for about 15 minutes, I asked the students if they understood the material, and if they had any questions so far. One girl raised her hand and asked "But who ARE you???" I immediately wondered to myself how anyone could ask such a question! I then responded "Isn't this Bio 120, section SXD????" The entire class said "NOOOOOOO"! Then I realized I was in the WRONG class! Apparently the professor who taught THAT class was also LATE—even LATER than me! Feeling 'MAAAAD' STUPID AND EMBARASSED, I tried to save face, by grabbing my belongings and walking out and saying "I did that PURPOSELY, just as a JOKE"! They immediately responded, laughing "YEAH, YEAH, ---RIGHT"! Then I walked further down the hall to my CORRECT class, and luckily, they were still there, waiting!

PROFESSORS FROM HELL!

EXAMPLE 1: THE 'SCREAMING MANIAC' BIOLOGY PROFESSOR

I was taking an undergraduate biology course many years ago (the university, course title, and professor's name shall remain nameless!). On the first day of class, the professor handed out a set of rules, and he explained that you can only talk to him during his office hours, and that if you had a question about how your exam was graded, you must see your laboratory instructor first. He did not want to be bothered with students outside of his office ours, nor especially with questions about one's exam grades. I didn't care about his STUPID rules! As a student, I felt I had a 'RIGHT' to see him and question him about grades! So one day I went to his office and knocked on his door. He said "Yes?", and I entered the room while he was working on some research papers he was writing. "Is there any way I can find out how I did on the test?", I asked. In an INSTANT, that ASS-HOLE began SCREAMING at the top of his lungs "GET OUT OF HERE!!!" It happened so fast that I didn't know what hit me! I never would have expected a professor---supposedly a 'professional' to act like a 'freaking MANIAC'! I then began to laugh, thinking this was some kind of joke! "I don't think that was very funny" he responded. My answer was "I just wanted to find out how I did on the test", I replied. He answered, "at the beginning of the course, you were given a paper with a set of rules, explaining that I am only available during office hours, and that you have to see your lab instructor about exam grades FIRST!" I told him, that I never received any such paper (which was a total LIE on my part). "Well maybe you weren't at the lecture when the paper was given out", he said. "O, sorry", I replied, and left his office.

Actually, I knew damn well about his STUPID rules and I did indeed receive the paper, but I felt that I was paying tuition, and who the HELL was HE to act like a total screaming LUNATIC to a student! The problem was that he was still the professor and he would still have to give me a final grade, so I didn't file a complaint with the department chairman (another 'wise-ass'!). But in retrospect, I should right then and there have told him that he was a freaking ASSHHOLE, and that it was too bad he already ad tenure, otherwise I would see to it that he would be filing for unemployment! But if I were to ever meet him on the street, I will tell him EXCACTLY what I think of him (even though he is now probably retired, if even still 'vertical')! I also found out later on that other students who dared to violate his 'rules' were treated the same way. Sometimes 'TENURE' is NOT a good thing! The purpose of tenure is to protect 'academic freedom', not "ASS-HOLE FREEDOM" as was HIS case!

EXAMPLE 2: PROFESSOR "UUUUUUUHHHHHHHHH"!

I was taking an undergraduate English course, and the professor was a real NUT JOB! It was during the summer session, and the class had over 25 students. Every day, at the beginning of class, she would take attendance by the roll-call method. She would read off the students' names, one by one, but after every name she would say "UUUUUUUUHHHHHHHHHH"! I could understand an occasional "UUUUUHHHHHH" after calling a dozen or so names, just as a pause, but after EVERY name???? For example, she would say "Mr. Smith,

UUUUUUUUHHHHH, Mr. Jones,

UUUUUUUUHHHHHHHH, Mr. Ross,

UUUUUUUUUUHHHHHHH, Miss Hathaway,

UUUUUUUUUHHHHHHH, Miss Springer,

UUUUUUUUUHHHHHHH, Mr. Nobleman,

UUUUUUUUHHHHHHHHH.........." This went on and on until every one of the 25 or 30 names were called, and it went on every day, day after day, week after week! This woman was a total NUT JOB, and probably three quarters of the class received D's or even F's in the course! She dressed in crappy clothes, and she was always telling the class stories about behavior problems she was having with her 3-year-old daughter (like anybody really cared!). At the end of the course, many students complained about her, myself included! I never saw her teaching a class at the college again after that! Like 'Captain Gulliver', who only wanted his 'due', she really GOT her due!

EXAMPLE 3: THE PROFESSOR WHO WOUND UP 'ALL WET'!

I would not say that this next professor, whom I had for a graduate class, was "from Hell'---he wasn't a bad guy, but since we're talking about professors, I'd like to tell you a great story! It was a small class, only about a dozen students, and the professor was telling us that earlier that day, he was sitting in his office, writing some papers, when suddenly a pipe in the ceiling above his office BURST! He told us that water began spewing out of the pipe and through the ceiling like a WATERFALL. He said, "I was sitting in my office, at my desk, when suddenly a pipe in the ceiling BURST, and all the water came down and ruined all of my papers and the books on my desk!" Upon hearing those words, the other students in the class were silent and sympathetic, but I BURST OUT LAUGHING! To me, that was HILARIOUS! For the next two hours, as he was lecturing, I couldn't hold in the laughter (although I tried to hide it!). To this day, and as I'm writing this story), every time I think about it, I become HYSTERICAL! The professor probably thought I was some kind of 'NUT JOB" (which admittedly, I AM)!

"FOOD FIIIIIIIIIIIIIIIIIGHT!!!"

It was my first year teaching in the NYC school system, and I was teaching 7th grade science in a junior high school. Experienced teachers will tell you that teaching junior high school is the WORST, because at that age, the kids are undergoing puberty and the "hormones are RAGING"!

It was the day just before the Christmas holiday, and the administration gave teachers a choice: We could either dismiss our official class early, about 1 PM, or we could hold a holiday 'party' in their classroom from 1 to 3 PM, after which the kids would be dismissed. Of course, the school would not provide the candy and refreshments from the school's money, so any teachers electing to have a party would have to buy and bring in their own candy and refreshments. I chose to have a party, and I bought plenty of candy, gum, cookies, lollipops and soda and brought it in with me on that 'party' day. Earlier that day, the deans told me that the party would be boring, because the kids did not have any social life at that age, and they would just be sitting at their desks quietly, eating the candy, and not conversing at all with their fellow classmates. I told the deans that it didn't matter, because in the holiday spirit, the kids probably would appreciate me more for making the 'party'---(or so I THOUGHT)!

Again, as the deans warned, I expected the kids to be seated quietly at their desks eating the candy and talking very little. I assumed the deans would be correct because, after all, they were deans and had many more years of experience than I did!

The 'party' started out exactly as the deans predicted---the kids sitting in their seats quietly eating the candy and lollipops, and I thought to myself "boy—these deans really know their stuff—they really know these kids!". After a few minutes, BOY were THEY WRONG"! First, a lollipop came zooming across the room, followed by another a few seconds later, followed by another, then ANOTHER, then ANOTHER! Then, COOKIES starting flying across the room, then GUM, then chocolate candy, then peppermint sticks----the room was like a shooting gallery! There was NOISE all over the place—yelling, screaming, kids running around, jumping up and down all over the place! It was like a scene from "ANIMAL HOUSE" with JOHN BELUSH! I had to 'duck and cover' to prevent getting hit, and that was also true of the kids (even though it was THEY that were shooting the candy! After a few more minutes, the PRINCIPAL opened the door, and yelled "WHAT'S GOING ON HERE?" (as if he didn't know)! Realizing he had no control over the situation, he closed the door and went on his way! After that day, I learned "NO MORE HOLIDAY PARTIES! NO MORE PARTIES OF ANY KIND!!!

MUSICAL CHAIRS
(WITHOUT THE MUSIC)!

I was visiting my aunt and uncle who lived in the Coney Island section of Brooklyn, and they told me that later that evening, some friends from Florida who were currently visiting relatives in Brooklyn would be coming over this evening to visit for a few hours. When it got close to their arrival time, my aunt asked me to bring a few extra chairs from the closet to the dining room table so we could all sit and chat over coffee and cake. But she told me NOT to bring over a certain chair, because that particular chair originally belonged to the visitor and that she borrowed it from her in the past but forgot to return it to her. She was worried that the guest would recognize that it was actually HER chair and my aunt would feel awkward for not returning it. When the guest arrived, with her husband and another friend, my aunt realized that we would need more chairs, so she asked me to go into the closet and find a couple more chairs to bring over. My uncle, who was in another room, gave me THAT chair to bring in, but I told him that my aunt previously told me NOT to bring in THAT particular chair. But I guess he didn't believe me, or thought I didn't know what I was talking about, so he told me to bring in THAT chair anyway! So I grabbed THAT chair and brought it into the dining room, and my aunt told me, in front of her guests, NOT to bring THAT chair, making an excuse that it was too small. So now I took THAT chair back to the closet. My uncle, seeing me bringing back THAT chair, told me, again, to bring THAT chair to the dining room table again, but I told him, a second time, that my aunt said "NO!". Again, he said, "BRING IN THAT CHAIR!", So I brought THAT chair to the dining room table AGAIN! At that point, my aunt told me, again, "DON'T BRING IN THAT CHAIR"! This went on a few more times, so finally I brought THAT chair to the table, hoping the guest would not recognize it as her original property! The guest never said anything about it, so either she completely forgot it was HER original chair, or she didn't WANT to remember that it was originally hers! I guess I'll never know the answer to that question!

"MOM, DAD……DID YOU KNOW THAT MY SHOES CRAWLED UNDER THE RADIATOR, AND RJ WAS ON *TELEVISION* !!!!

I had an aunt and uncle and three cousins who lived not far from me---about a mile away, so we and our parents visited each other occasionally. One Saturday night, our parents went out on the town, so they decided I would stay over at their (my cousins'), house, since I was only about 10 years old, and I was the kind of kid who they did NOT want to leave 'home alone' (and I wonder why)! While I was there, one of my cousins took off his shoes to lie on the couch and watch TV, and when he wasn't looking, I took his shoes and brought them into the next room and hid them under the radiator! A little later, while they were all watching TV, I stood in front of the TV, making believe I was actually performing on the show! But they were NOT impressed! A little later my cousin began looking for his shoes, but couldn't find them. After a while, I 'volunteered' to help him look for them, and I 'mysteriously' found them under the radiator!' I showed my cousin where the shoes were, and he took them back and put them on! "Gee-I wonder HOW they got there", I said. He replied, "Yea---I WOONDER---they must have crawled under their themselves"! We both agreed that strange things do sometimes just "HAPPEN"! When his parents came home, he told them "Mom, Dad……. did you know that my shoes crawled under the radiator, and RJ was on TELEVISION"!!! Well, all I can say is that THAT was the last time I was invited to stay over their house when the parents spent another night on the town! Probably just a 'coincidence'???????

DOIN' THE PEACH PIT (W)RAP)!

I had two male cousins, who, when they were teenagers, managed to get a part-time summer job preparing sandwiches and lunch boxes for the homeless (or whomever wanted a free prepared lunch package) at a nearby food pantry. The sandwiches and dessert fruits and other items were packaged and out into small packages which were later given out to those in need and/or whoever came to the site to receive them. One cousin, on particular, was kind of a 'wise-guy' and 'joker', who always did some very stupid things as jokes, which in HIS mind were 'funny'! One day they were wrapping up peaches in plastic wrap and adding them to the lunch package, and he noticed that some peaches were very ripe and were actually staring to split open. So this joker decided to pull out the pit, then wrap the pit in plastic wrap, then put the wrapped pit BACK into the peach, then he wrapped the entire peach up with more plastic wrap, and placed it in the lunch package. Whoever got those lunch packages must have really wondered HOW the peach PIT inside the peach got wrapped, as well as the entire peach!

NO SENSE CRYING OVER SPILLED WATER! (or) HER GLASS RUNNETH OVER!

When I was about 15 years old, an aunt of mine and an uncle of mine (named Jack) (not married to each other but married to another aunt and uncle) came over for a visit one evening, as they often did. They were sitting at the dining room table with my father, engaged in conversation and possibly playing a card game. My aunt asked me to bring her a glass of water, which she promptly put at her side on the table. My uncle often wore a cap, and often did so at the table. Apparently, after a while, he took off his cap and put it beside himself on the table, and somehow after a while longer the cap fell down, lying upside down, which neither he nor anyone else noticed. A short time later, my aunt accidently spilled her glass of water, and asked me to get her some napkins so she could wipe the water off the tablecloth before it spilled onto the floor. As I handed her the napkins, I noticed that most of the water had already SPILLED off the tablecloth onto the floor. Upon closer examination, I noticed the water spilled not only onto the floor, but INTO MY UNCLE'S HAT, which was lying upside down on the floor! "AH HAH HAH HAAAAAAAAH!!!" I shouted, "LOOK---the water spilled off the table right onto uncle Jack's HAT!!!". Uncle Jack looked, then picked up the hat, said NOTHING, and just began to STARE at it—noting that it was now SOAKED from the inside out! We all became HYSTERICAL (especially ME)!!!

CAN WE PLEEEEEASE GET THE VOCALIST OUT OF HERE!!!

My second dog, (and my first Basset Hound's) name was Axelrod—(it is a boy's name, but she was a girl). Anyway, sometimes I used to tease/play with her by singing in front of her, or HOWLING! She would respond by howling herself, like a wolf—"OWWWWOOOOOOOOOOOOOOH"! I think we've seen many TV shows where dogs would howl when their owners sang and/or played the piano! Elvis used to sing for HIS dog too!

Anyway, when I was in high school, (only a few blocks away from my home), I was in the school concert band. A few times a year we put on concerts in the school auditorium, mostly during the holiday seasons. The conductor, my music teacher, whom I knew from junior high school (let's call him "Mr. C), was a nice guy, musically very talented, but a bit of a 'wack', if you know what I mean! Anyway, one year, before the holidays, we were preparing for a concert. We had to rehearse extra hours, so during 'Spring Break', he arranged for the school to be open for the band members, to allow us extra hours to rehearse. Since school was officially closed, the scenario was very informal, and even Mr. C brought is DOG to school, and when the band was rehearsing, he put his dog by himself to rest in one of the practice rooms. It seemed to me that Mr. C was just trying to show-off his dog to the band (although, admittedly, it was a nice, friendly, well-behaved dog!). I guess I became jealous, and wanted the band to see MY dog as well, so I went home and brought my dog in too! Everybody was admiring her, saying what a nice, well-behaved dog she was, admiring her long tail, cow-like colors, and long, floppy ears!

There was no more space in the practice room, so I tied her to a table with her leash and the band began to play the songs we were going to perform. As the band played, she began to HOWL! (And if you don't know the voice of a basset Hound, it is maaaaaaadddd LOUD!). So as we played, and she began to HOWL like crazy--- the band members became hysterical and had a hard time to continue playing! Mr. C stopped the band from playing, and shouted "Can we PLEEEEEEEASE get the VOCALIST out of here"! So I took her home and returned a few minutes later!

WASHING-MACHINE BLUES!

When I was about 7 years old, I had a FASCINATION with washing machines! I don't know the reason for it, but I was obsessed with watching the machine go round and round and round! I was especially fascinated during the spinning cycle, and watching the water shoot out of the drain pump!

Across the street from my house, there was a laundry mat. Every day, before and after school, I would enter it and watch the dozen or more washing machines wash clothes, go on the spin, watch the waste water exit trough the rubber pump, then go on the rinse and repeat the entire cycle! In the morning, my mother would have to go into the laundry mat to force me go to school! One day, as I was staring at the machine, some water, containing soap and bleach splashed out of the tub and into my face! That was the last time I went into THAT laundry mat!

One day my mother had to go shopping, so she brought me to my aunt Sally's house to be baby sited for a few hours. Aunt Sally had a washing machine in her basement, and she started doing her wash—she probably did it right then to keep me quiet! Her machine was an upright – loading machine, but if you opened the cover, it would stop working temporarily, as a safety measure, until the top cover was closed again. Once the top was closed, it would re-start. Aunt Sally told me not to open the top for that reason, and then she went back upstairs. As for me, I kept opening the top cover many times (it was no fun to watch the washing machine wash unless the top cover was open and you could actually see it work)! Every time I opened the top cover, the machine would stop, and aunt Sally would hear it stop, and would scream out (from upstairs) "RJ---DON'T OPEN THE TOP COVER!" So I would close it again and have my fun for a few minutes, then opened it again, and the screaming cycle would be repeated (MANY MANY TIMES!).

There was another laundry mat a few blocks away from my home (with only front-loading machines) and I would often go there as well to watch them work. Sometimes, the users would add to much detergent, and water and soap would exit from the top of the machine, onto the floor! Sometimes, when that happened, the whole floor would get flooded, and the patron would have to use a mop to mop up the mess! I LOVED IT when that happened, and would become hysterical and laugh in their face while they were mopping up the mess! You should have seen how EMBARRASSED they were (and how STUPID they must have felt---which I could tell from the LOOK on their face)!

"ONLY THE NOSE KNOWS!"

When I was in junior high school, I had a music teacher who all the kids liked, and was a relatively nice guy, but a bit 'wacky'! One thing funny that he used to do was to grab a kid's nostrils (gently), at which point the kid was supposed to say "only the nose knows", and the teacher would release the kid's nostrils! This was taken all in fun!

Anyway, speaking of noses, I had a close friend who I often went with to neighborhood restaurants. For some reason, every time we began eating, he always developed mucus ('snot') in his nose, and obviously then he had to blow his nose. The problem was that when he blew his nose, the restaurant (which was quiet with all the people eating), had to HEAR him blowing is nose! He was a bit over-weight, and when he blew his nose, it sounded like a large cruise ship that was about to sail! (Or like a locomotive blowing its' HORN!) Everyone in the restaurant could hear him blow his nose, and it sounded like a foghorn! But they also heard the 'snot' going into the tissue, which made it all the more DISGUSTING, especially while people were eating! Sometimes, when he didn't have tissues, he would use the cloth napkin or bib that the restaurant provided when they had set the table (which made it even MORE DISGUSTING! His nose blowing was so loud, that every time he blew it, I would yell out "all ABOARD"! To make matters worse, even the waiter would come over and tell him to stop blowing his nose, or he would ask him to go OUTSIDE and blow his nose THERE! And, when he blew his nose INSIDE the restaurant, (which he ALWAYS did), I would yell out "DISGUSTING!" Then I would make a face (of HORROR) and yell out "EEEEEEEEWWWWWW, EEEEEEEEWWWWWWW, EEEEEEEEEWWWWWWW!!!". It reached a point that every time we entered the restaurant in the future, the waiter would warn him not to blow his nose, or to go outside FIRST and blow is nose THERE, before we could be seated! (The problem with THAT was that he usually didn't develop snot until he began the meal, so he had no reason to blow it at that point)! Then I would ask the waiter, jokingly, "what's six feet long, green, and hangs from a tree?" The answer: "ELEPHANT SNOT"!!! (an old joke). The waiter, however, didn't seem amused!

JUMPIN' IN DA 'HOOD'! ------(or)---- WHO'S BEEN JUMPING IN MYYYYY HOOD?

I was in a small neighborhood restaurant during lunchtime one day. The tables were arranged such that if you were sitting on one side, all you could see was the counter and cash register, but if you were sitting on the other side, you could see outside the front window at the street and traffic and parked cars in front of the restaurant. I was seated on the side were you could see the street and traffic and parked cars. A block or so away was a small lumber yard. All of a sudden, I saw about three adult men running, and I recognized two of them as lumber yard workers, although I did not know them personally, but I did not recognize the third guy. Apparently, these guys involved in some kind of fight, with the two lumber yard workers chasing after the third guy. What the fight was about I had no idea---I just assumed the third guy was an unhappy customer, but it could have been some other reason. Next thing I knew, one of the lumber yard workers picked up a large, netted metal city garbage can and JUMPED on top of the hood of one of the parked cars with it! He held the garbage can up in attempt to THROW the can at the third guy! The third guy, seeing the danger, ran away, and the two lumber yard workers ran back to the lumber yard. Apparently, the fight, or impending fight, was over! "BOY! That was STRANGE!" I thought to myself. It was as if I was in a 'lunch theatre' (as opposed to a dinner theatre), and that entire scenario was for my entertainment! I had never seen such a scenario before and thought it was MAAAAAAAD FUNNY---which it WAS! That seemed to be the end of the 'show'! When I left the restaurant, I looked at the car whose hood the combatant stood on with the garbage can. I noticed that the entire hood was CAVED in!!! I can't IMAGINE WHAT the owner of that CRUSHED parked car must have thought when he returned to start is car! He probably thought that somebody dropped an ELEPHANT on it! What ever happened after that or whether he (or she) reported it to the police, I never found out---(but I certainly decided NEVER to park MY car there!!!).

RJ, YOU HAVE A *WAY* WITH BIRDS!"

One summer I was taking a two-week field course called "Arctic Ecosystems" in Churchill, Manitoba, Canada, which is known as the polar bear capitol of the world! While we did spot some polar bears in the distance, we never got too close to them to be in any real danger. The professors (about 4 of them) always guided the students in the field with rifles, just in case we accidently stepped over a polar bear resting in the bushes (in the Willows).

One day, while the class was walking through the fields, we spotted a large, black bird on the branch of a nearby tree. The bird was about the size of a crow. I was munching on an apple at the time, and decided I would hold the core part in my fingers and held it up to the bird (who was about 20 feet away on the branch), just to see what, if anything, the bird would do (in other words, whether the bird would fly near me to try to get the food). Upon seeing the apple core, the bird, unexpectedly, flew toward me, and landed in my chest and face! It happened so fast that I didn't even realize what happened, and I held on to the apple core; then the bird flew away! Another student, seeing this said "RJ, you're SUPPOSED to let it (the food) GO!" But, like I said, the bird flew into my face so fast that I didn't have time to react! Then the other student said "RJ, You have a *WAY* with *BIRDS*!" I was hoping the bird would return to get the apple core, but it flew away instead! So I tossed the apple core away in the field. Who knows---maybe there are now several apple trees growing there!

THE MALICIOUS, COMPULSIVE LIAR!

When I was about 11 years old, and in the sixth grade of elementary school, there was a kid about my age in one of my classes, ---we'll call him "Humphrey". Humphrey wasn't exactly my enemy, but he wasn't exactly my 'friend' either. But one thing I will say about Humphrey, he was a compulsive liar, and often a malicious liar as well! I remember one day when he rolled up a big spitball and threw it at the teacher while the teacher was sitting at his desk. The teacher did not actually SEE Humphrey throw the spitball, but he saw it come from Humphrey's direction. So he asked Humphrey, in front of the whole class if HE threw the spitball. Humphrey adamantly DENIED throwing the spitball, saying "I didn't throw it---I SWEAR, I SWEAR, I SWEAR---I didn't throw it!" But the teacher was convinced that Humphrey DID throw the spitball, and the dialog went back and forth several times, with Humphrey denying and SWEARING he didn't do it! Even Humphrey's best friend, seated next to him, testified that before the spitball was thrown, Humphrey showed it to him and asked him "Should I THROW it? ---should I THROW it?" (With BEST friends like THAT, WHO needs ENEMIES????). Anyway, the scenario ended there, as the teacher couldn't absolutely prove that Humphrey threw it (though he and I were SURE that he did!).

Anyway, one day, during lunch break, when me and another classmate (a friend of mine) were walking home (we were allowed to go home or lunch), I saw Humphrey walking across the street. I yelled to my classmate, loud enough for Humphrey to hear "AH HA HA HA HAAAAA---THERE'S HUMPHREY, THERE's HUMPHREY, AH HA HA HA HA HA.!!!". There was no malice intended, I just wanted Humphrey to know that I saw him across the street. Humphrey didn't respond, he just went on his way walking home, and we went on our merry way----the incident (I thought) was over!

When we returned to school about an hour later, me and my friend were in gym class, playing games and whatever. All of sudden, a student monitor approached me and told me that someone was waiting outside the gym and wanted to talk to me. I had no idea WHO it was, but I went out the door to find out. Who was there? It was the PRINCIPAL, accompanied by Humphrey. And Humphrey concocted some crazy story that during lunch-break, as he was walking home from school, me and another kid saw Humphrey across the street, and we started THROWING ROCKS at him! I told the principal that no such thing happened, and that I merely saw Humphrey across the street, and since I knew him, just yelled out "AH HA HA HA… there's Humphrey, there's Humphrey", and that NOBODY threw any rocks at him! The conversation ended there. But to this day, I still wonder why Humphrey concocted such a story! I guess that it will just be one of those 'Unsolved Mysteries'! After that incident, I just kind of completely ignored Humphrey, although in high school he was in some of my classes again. LUCKY ME!!!!!!!!

THE SUN, GRRRRRRRRRRRADUATION, AND 'BIG MIKE'!

When I taught high school science (biology, chemistry, and Earth science), I always liked to tell jokes. Most of the jokes were not really funny, and most were also very 'CORNY'! 'Big Mike' was a student in my class—kind of a GIANT! He must have been 6 foot five, and weighed about 300 pounds! He had a friendly, jolly personality, and always laughed at my jokes, not only to get a passing grade, but also because he had a great sense of humor, even when my jokes were corny (which was almost ALL of the time!). When he laughed, the entire building SHOOK—like there was an earthquake! The entire building trembled when he laughed, and his laugh could probably bust your ear drums! I think he might have had to stay an extra term before he could graduate in order to make up some missed classes. I loved having him in my classes, because he 'livened and spiced them up, so that the other students would not fall asleep (and probably so that I WOULD NOT PUT MYSELF TO SLEEP AS WELL!).

One day, in Earth science, I was covering the unit on astronomy, and I was discussing supernovas (exploding stars). I taught that all stars eventually burn out their hydrogen fuel supply, and die out, usually by exploding (a supernova). After exploding, all that is usually left behind is a cloud of gas, called a "nebula". Sometimes, out of this nebula, new, smaller stars are born. And I noted that all stars are actually suns, and all suns are actually stars, our sun included! I explained that, as a typical star, our sun will probably also explode some day, forming a supernova, but that scientists tell us that it will probably not happen for another 4 to 5 billion years or so. That means that the sun, and our planet and solar system, will still be around for another 4 or 5 billion years, and then "CAPUT"! I then asked the students if they should worry about that, since 5 billion years is kind of a LONG TIME from now! All the students raised their and said "NO" when I asked "how many of you are going to worry about that?" Then I made one of my corny jokes, by saying "well, you SHOULD worry about that, and when they asked "WHY?", I responded, "Because that's just about the time, that MANY of you, if not MOST of you, if not ALL of you, will be GRRRRRRRRADUATING!!!!", and I said that in a high pitch, as I generally do when I tell my jokes! (Although I'm not sure if it was really a "joke"!) 'BIG Mike' got the joke right away, and began his ear-drum' blasting laugh! The building began to SHAKE---and everyone in the building knew that it was NOT an earthquake, it was just 'Big Mike' laughing at one of my CORNY jokes!

A SHIRT OF MANY COLORS!
(GEEEEE, THANNNNNNKS!")

When I was about 10 years old, I was still a SLOB! I hardly ever washed my hands or face, I used to spit on the floor, I often picked my nose and rolled the buggers (cootsies) between my fingers, I would sneeze and wipe the snot away using my sleeves, among other 'slobbish' things! One day, one of my teachers in an after-school program told me "YOU are the worst slob ever! You are annoying, disgusting, you have no manners and no class whatsoever! I've never met a 'SLOB' or PIG like you among the many students I've ever had in my classes" Then he continued to berate me (actually, it was not "berating me since it was the TRUTH!) for about another ten minutes! After he finished berating me, he became silent, waiting to hear what my response would be. My response: "GEEEEEEEE! THANNNNNNNNNNKS!". In the bible, there is the story of Joseph, who was famous for having a coat of many different colors. As the SLOB I was that I spoke about above, one day I came to class with a shirt of many colors---but NOT because it was designed that way, but rather because whenever I ate, I would wipe my fingers and hands on the nearest available 'napkin', which was usually my SHIRT! So when I came to class (late, as usual), all the other kids were hysterical and began to tell me, like the teacher, what a SLOB I was and how 'GROSS' and DISGUSTING my shirt was! Rather than acknowledge that they were right, I tried to tell them that this was a new style of shirt, ---a new design----and that I actually bought the shirt that way! Believe me, they did not BUY that explanation!

"RJ----CAN YOU PLEASE GO OUTSIDE AND FIND OUT WHY THE BABY'S CRYING?"

When I was a kid, I was a real "Dennis the Menace"! One day an aunt of mine came over to visit. A few years earlier she had given birth to a baby boy, so now I had a cousin only three years younger than me. I was about 5 and he was about 2. When his mother came over one summer day, she sat in my living room chatting with my mother, and the baby carriage with my baby cousin was right outside our window. I liked to tease at the time (and still do so now!). So while the adults were chatting, I went outside and stood in front of the carriage. Then, I said to my baby cousin, in a Frankenstein-like tone, and with Frankenstein-like gestures "Your mother is on the traaaaaain (subway), and she's going FAR FAAAAAARRRRR AWAAAAAAY---and she's not coming **BACK!**". Then my cousin would start to cry. I don't think he even understood what I said, but from my Frankenstein-like tone and gestures, I'm SURE I scared him! Then I calmly walked back into my house. Then my aunt asked me "RJ—can you please go outside and find out why the baby's crying?" So I innocently went outside, then I came back in and told my aunt that I didn't know why the baby was crying! A few weeks later, they came to visit again, and I did the same thing! Then my aunt heard me and told my cousin not to listen to me!

Y'AH POOOOOOOP!

Regarding my cousin in the baby carriage who I scared and made him cry, a year or so later I was at his parents new home in Long Island, and we were sitting on his back porch playing with his toy trucks. I was about 7 years old and he was about 3 years old. As he was showing me his toy trucks, I (again as a "Dennis the Menace") began messing the trucks up, on purpose! He kept getting annoyed, and the more he got annoyed, the more I messed his trucks up! Eventually, every time I messed up his trucks, he got mad and called me "y'AH POOP!" I didn't know what exactly a "Poop" is, but I knew it wasn't anything nice! And I continued to mess up his trucks, and he kept saying "Y'AH POOP! Y'AH POOOP! Y'AH POOOP!". Eventually he called me an "ALLEY POOP"! Exactly what a Poop was I did not know, and exactly what an "Alley Poop" was I did not know either! But after that day, whenever I visited him again, he never invited me to help him play with his toy trucks (nor ANY of his toys) again!

CAT ON A HOT TIN MOTOR!

When I was a kid, probably around eight years old, I fed a lot of stray cats in the neighborhood---we called them "alley cats", because they often hung around people's alleys. One day I was walking on my block, and some guy was working on is car, with the hood open. Apparently, after he opened the hood and walked away for a few moments, one of these alley cats jumped under the hood and sat on top of the motor (which luckily was off). The guy saw me and knew of my cat association, and he called me over and asked "Can you get this cat out of my engine?" I said "Yes", because I didn't think it was such a big deal, and I walked over and picked up the cat. Immediately, the cat jumped out of arms and fled the scene, but not before scratching up the entire top of the palm of my hand! I don't mean a few scratches---the whole top of the palm of my hand was scratched! I took a neighbor's garden hose and washed it off, but the pain was awful! But I didn't tell or show it to anybody---not even to the guy who asked me to get the cat out of the engine in the first place! A few days later, my mother saw the scratches and asked me how I got them. I told her the story about how the guy asked me to get the cat out of under his hood, and the cat scratched me! She told me "Next time the guy asks you to get the cat out of his car, tell him to DO IT HIMSELF!

NO FREE COFFEE!

Some years ago I was on a bus tour, somewhere out west, and the bus was fairly full. Amongst the other tourists was an elderly couple—a man and his wife who I became friendly with. The bus driver stopped at numerous restaurants and coffee shops for meals and snacks and for the use of restrooms. One place we stopped at was a small luncheonette, where we could buy drinks, snacks, coffee, sodas, etc. The wife complained about the coffee, saying it looked HORRIBLE! She said it looked like MUD! My response to her was "of course it looks like MUD---it was just GROUND this morning!". Whether she got the pun or not I do not know---my guess is she probably did not, because she did not seem exactly like a GENIUS! Then she repeated, "that coffee looks like MUD---I wouldn't drink it if you gave it to me for NOTHING!" My response to her was "OK, so next time I'll CHARGE you for it---THEN you'll DRINK it!". She probably still didn't get the pun!

"INSTANT SHMUCK IDENTIFICATION!"

Getting back to my friend John Doe, one day we went to a TV show taping in Manhattan. After the show, we decided to go for breakfast in a nearby restaurant. When we went to the counter to pay the bill, we each paid separately. I approached the cashier (a nice young pretty girl) first, and I paid my check and she handed me the change. At that point, I noticed on the counter that there was a dish of free mints, so I told John---"OH WOW! MINTS! I really like mints, especially when they're FREE!" Upon saying that, I grabbed a whole HANDFUL for myself and put them in my coat pocket! Upon seeing that, the cashier made a gesture to John, twirling her ringer around her ear, that I was CRAZY (and I WAS! —and still am!). John, standing on line right next to me, then laughed and paid HIS bill (but took only ONE free mint). Upon leaving the restaurant, John said to me "You see----even the CASIHER knows what a NUT JOB you are---and SHE never even SAW you before! Yah' know what that's called? That's called instant SHMUCK identification!".

"THANK YOU FOR PLAYING THE TROMBONE"
Brought to You By
THE PRINCIPAL FROM HELL!

I had a friend, let's call him Jon Doe, who received his Master's degree in special education, and he landed a job as a high school special education teacher. I'm not going to tell you what school it was, nor the city, not even the state it was in. The principal, known for being a real SOB, especially by new and untenured teachers, like my friend John, liked to pick on the weak---those teachers who could easily be fired, and those teachers whose lives he could make MISERABLE! Anyway, this principal was always observing John Doe, and was always ready to write John up for the least little petty things—any and every petty little thing he could think of! He would often belittle John, in writing. For example, on one observation report he told John, in writing, "Your clothes are too tight for your person", basically calling him fat, as John was a bit on the 'stocky' side. This was many years ago. If this happened today, that principal would be immediately FIRED and sued for $ MILLIONS!

As another example, John was team teaching a special education class in the same room with another teacher. One day the other teacher needed an item from an office that he forgot to bring to class with him. That teacher asked John, his team teaching colleague, to go downstairs to the office to pick up the item he needed. So John obliged, but on the way back to the classroom, John spotted the principal at the other end of the hallway, and the principal spotted John at the same time. So John started running back to the classroom so the principal would not catch him out of the classroom, and the principal began running through the hallway after John! John made it back to the classroom before the principal did, but the next day the principal wrote John up for not being in his classroom. In that letter, the principal stated that he saw John in the hall, out of his classroom, and that he (the principal ran after him; and even though he did not actually catch John, he knew it was John! I told John to rebut the write-up, and that he should state in the rebuttal letter that "nobody should run through the halls, teacher, student, or principal, because running through the halls is dangerous!" And, to his credit, Join did indeed add that to the rebuttal letter!

To show you what an SOB that principal from HELL was, one day the school band was performing a concert for the student body in the school auditorium. John was a great musician himself, playing several instruments, especially the tuba, the baritone horn, and the trombone. The school band was rather small, so a number of teachers who were also musicians volunteered to perform in the concert with the student members of the band. This took several days and many additional unpaid hours, often after school hours, of rehearsing, and John, a gifted musician, volunteered as well, by playing the trombone. After the concert was over (and it was a success!), the principal wrote letters of appreciation to ALL BUT ONE of the teachers who volunteered. The letter thanked them for their performance in the concert, expressing how deeply appreciated their voluntary service was, and how true professionals they really were, donating their time and musical talent! And, (YOU GUESSED IT), that one teacher who did NOT get that appreciation letter was JOHN! When John found out that all the other teachers who performed got that letter, EXCEPT HIM, John was PISSED! He began bitching and complaining about it, (AND RIGHTFULLY SO!) He kept repeating to everyone that all the other teachers who volunteered received appreciation letters in their mailboxes from the principal, and that JOHN should have also received a letter from the principal thanking him for playing the trombone!

Apparently, the principal got word of John's complaint through the 'grapevine'. So the next day, John received a letter in his mailbox from the principal as well, stating "Dear Mr. Doe: Thank you for playing the trombone". That was the entire letter! This is absolute PROOF, in my opinion, of what an SOB that principal from HELL really was! It showed his true colors! And, to prove the truth of the WHEEL of KARMA, a couple of years later the principal left the school to take on a better-paying job in another town, in another school district, and received a two year contract, which might be renewed after it expires. When the two years were up, the school district REFUSED to renew his contract, thereby FIRING HIS ASS! It just goes to show you, "what GOES around, COMES around"!!!

CHIM CHIMINEY, CHIM CHIMINEY, AND THE 'GENIUS' NEXT DOOR!

I live on a block of private but attached houses, all with backyards. For decades in the past, owners could not legally add extensions to their homes into their backyards, nor could they add additional floors upward nor downward. Over the past decade, the laws changed, and many of my neighbors began to legally extend their homes into their backyards. The neighbor on one side also extended his home, and called a construction company to do the job. A few years ago we had a very rainy summer, and water kept getting into his basement. He couldn't figure out WHERE the water was coming from (aside from the rain). Eventually he ASSUMED (we should NEVER "A-S-S-U-M-E"!) it was coming from the rain that entered our shared chimney. In his vast ingenuity and great use of Solomon's wisdom, he came up with a solution. He put a thick tarp over the chimney one rainy summer, thinking it would solve the flooding problem (I did not go up on the roof to inspect it), yet water continued to flood his basement after every strong rainstorm. One day my TV reception was going haywire, so I asked my handyman to check the roof and fix the antenna. After checking and adjusting the antenna, he came back down and asked me WHO put the tarp over the chimney. I explained that my next door neighbor did it to prevent flooding from the rain. He told me that after adjusting the antenna, he REMOVED the tarp, and said that we (my neighbor and I) were both very lucky that this happened during the summer (when little or no heat was used), because if it happened during the winter, when heat would be used, the houses would be filled with smoke and, worse—CARBON MONOXIDE-----in which case I would probably NOT be writing this story right now! By the way, the neighbor later found out that the water came from cracks in the foundation caused by cheap construction materials!

THE "BEAR-INARIAN"!

In the 1980', I took some summer field courses in volcanic and geothermal geology in Yellowstone National Park. These were great field courses! The professors drove the class around in vans where we visited Old Faithful and dozens of other geysers and hot springs, boiling mud pots and fumaroles (steam vents), ancient volcanic mudflows (lahars) and ancient lava flows, and other volcanic landscapes! Teachers and geologists brought their children to these events as well. One family brought their two young kids—brothers—who were about 6 and 8 years old. As we rode around the park sightseeing, we often talked about seeing bears, and we occasionally did see some, luckily, from a DISTANCE! I, being a joker, told the two young brothers that I had a pet bear that I kept in the woods, and since they believed me, it made me tell them more and more lies about my pet bear! They asked me all kinds of questions about were in the forest the bear actually lives, how often do I visit him, what do I feed him, how big he is, how old he is, etc. As I was telling them these outrageous lies, we actually SAW a bear in the hills in the distance! I yelled out "HEY---that's MY BEAR"! The kids got really excited! Everyone in the van kept talking about the bear, then one kid yelled out "THAT'S RJ's BEAR"! Then the kids kept asking me MORE questions, and my classmates kept silent, as they were getting a 'KICK' out of the phony stories! Then one kid asked me "what happens when your bear gets sick?" My answer was "When he gets SICK, I take him to a BEAR-inarian!" My classmates chuckled as I invented a NEW word! A "Bear-INARIAN", by my definition, is a veterinarian who specializes in treating bears (in case you are confused!). After we returned back to the classroom, one of my colleagues said to me, laughing, "BOY! Your CREDIBILITY really

SKYROCKETED when we actually SAW the bear roaming around"! My answer to him (a grown man) was "what do you MEAN my credibility SKYROCKETED? ---that really WAS my BEAR!".

SKUNKS AWAAAAAAAAY!

I was vacationing with a friend at a hotel on the Catskills some years ago. For whatever reasons, there were only a handful of guests there at that time, but we didn't care because we were going to spend much of the time hiking and exploring the area. One morning, one of the guests, an elderly woman, began screaming for Mr. Shopps, the owner! "MISTER SHOPPS, MISTER SHOPPS! ---MISTER SHOPPS!" she screamed. Everybody came running to the kitchen to find out what happened, and we saw the elderly woman running away from the kitchen door, with her hands covering her nose. What actually had happened was that when she looked out of the screen door, she saw a giant SKUNK standing there, peering inside! Frightened, she did what any GENIUS would do----she filled up a large pot of hot water from the sink and THREW it, right through the screen, right onto the skunk! The skunk, scared out of its wits and a bit annoyed, IMMEDIATELY SPRAYED, then ran away! We spent at least an hour hosing off the "PERFUME" that the skunk graciously 'donated' to us! I guess that skunk wasn't exactly in the mood for a hot water bath!

"BANQUET?????.........*WHAT* BANQUET?????"

I had a friend, let's call him "Sam". Sam was a relatively nice guy; at least he WANTED to be! He tried to be, and usually was, friendly, and would never hurt a fly. He graduated college, although it took him a little extra time, and eventually earned a Masters degree in special education. His main problem was that he wasn't exceptionally sharp in ordinary, day-to-day common sense. He held several different jobs, but none for too long. His father worked as a type of technician for a large New York City hotel chain.

Sam convinced his father to get him a job in a hotel, and started out as a "page". A page's main job is to communicate messages between staff members, often messages that are important. One day one of the hotel executives gave him a letter to bring to the hotel's head chef. The letter informed the chef that the following day, the hotel will be preparing a lunch-time banquet for 250 people, and the banquet was to start at 1:00 PM, promptly. The executive handed the letter to Sam and told him to give it personally to the head chef, in his HAND! He told Sam that it must be delivered personally, and that if he couldn't find the head chef in the kitchen, he must look for him throughout the hotel and make sure he handed it to him personally.

Sam couldn't find the head chef in the kitchen, so, as instructed, he searched for him throughout the hotel. He searched and searched for at least an hour, but to no avail! He searched kitchens, dining rooms, meeting rooms, the front desk, lounges, balconies, the business center, even the restrooms, but met with no success. After at least an hour, maybe two hours, of searching, Sam was frustrated and got tired. He decided to put the letter in the head chef's mailbox instead. Then he went on with his other chores.

The following morning, the executive in charge of the banquet phoned the head chef, and asked "So, is everything all set for the banquet this afternoon?" To which the head chef replied "BANQUET???? WHAT Banquet?????" To make a long story short, Sam was mailing out his resume, again, a short time later! (But, as for Sam, please understand that "he MEANT well)! (It just didn't always work OUT that way!!!).

"RJ, HAVEN'T YOU HAD ENOUGH?"

When I was a kid, here in Brooklyn there were several private cafeterias, where you could go through a line and choose your foods, and the cafeteria workers would add the food choice to your plate. The prices were usually very reasonable. After paying the cashier at the end of the line, you walked over with your tray to a table and ate your food. Sometimes these venues were very crowded, so you found yourself sharing a table with strangers; sometimes, an entire family picked a table for themselves. These cafeterias were very popular, but none still exist here anymore, at least none that I know of. We picked our dishes, put them on trays, paid at the cashier, and sat down at a table. I had a plate of French toast, a serving of which consisted of about 3 slices. Being the 'klutz' that I was, as I was eating, one of the French toast slices fell out of the plate, off the table, and onto the floor. I then picked it up, looked at it, and put it back on my plate. Then my mother said "RJ, haven't you had ENOUGH????" She, and my aunt and uncle thought I was going to eat it, even though it fell on the floor! Or maybe they thought that the slice was ALREADY on the floor from before, dropped by someone else. Honestly, I looked at it to see if it still looked clean, and it did! Whether I would really have eaten it, I don't know, BUT, knowing me and what a SLOB I was (and still AM), I probably WOULD HAVE!

"Z-Z-Z-Z-Z-Z-Z-Z-Z"! -or- TRYING TO BE RIP VAN WINKLE (IN CLASS)!

Several years ago I somehow developed severe sleep apnea. I would fall asleep just about anywhere, at any time, including dining room tables at friends' houses! It got so bad that my friends INSISTED I see a sleep disorder doctor! So I did! In order to diagnose my sleep apnea, they put all kinds of wires on my head and put some kind of 'goo" in my hair, and made me stay overnight with all kinds of wires and electrodes attached to my head! The next morning I was free to go home, and they told me to call for the results in a few days. It took HOURS for me to wash that krap out of my hair, and my head wound up looking like a porcupine for weeks! When I called for the results, I was told I had severe sleep apnea, and that overnight I had stopped breathing 92 times!

The only possible treatment, outside of surgery, was for me to put on that stupid bipop mask overnight. When I tried it out, I almost suffocated! I felt like I was connected to the exhaust end of a vacuum cleaner! (Like Ralph Kramden did on the Honeymooners!). Obviously, I chose not to use the mask and decided to just live with the condition.

Anyway, at that time I was also taking some college classes, just for the heck of it since I'm a 'professional student', currently having amassed probably 700 or more credits! The problem is that my sleep apnea causes me to fall asleep in class often, and, to make it worse, I usually SNORE, LOUDLY, on top of that! Many of my professors got (and still get) PISSED, because it interferes with their lectures and the other students' ability to concentrate or even HEAR the lecture! In addition, the professors get the impression that the reason I fall asleep in their classes is that I'm inferring that they're BORING (which sometimes really IS the case)! One professor got so pissed that he made me sign up with the "Students With Disabilities" office! That office told me that they did not consider sleep apnea a true disability, and that they could do nothing about it for me (nor the professors)! In another class, on the first day, I snored so loudly that the professor told me "this cannot continue! We have to do something about it---and, if necessary, (I would) have to drop the class". Another professor told me that during the class, "Boy!---you were sawing WOOD!". For the professor who told me that I would have to drop the class---I DID! As for the professor who told me that I was sawing wood, I started drinking several cups of regular coffee just before class, which seemed to have helped, at least somewhat!

Somehow my apnea has lessened since then, but not completely! I also think this was DISCRIMINATION against sleep apnea patients, and possibly BORING professors as well!

MRS. SHARP-ROCK!

Teaching junior high school, I believe, most teachers will tell you, is probably the worst age group to teach. Hormones are raging, and the kids, in general, are totally immature and out of control! I began teaching in a NYC junior high school, and it was 'BOOT-CAMP'! If you can get through one year at the junior high school level, you've 'made it' as a teacher!

The best way to handle disruptive kids is to call their parents. However, I have found that sometimes, after dealing with the parents, you can understand why the kids are the way they are! This is not the case for ALL of the kids, but it seems to be the rule rather than the exception!

Anyway, when I had a disruptive student, I would first tell the kid that if he or she doesn't behave, I would telephone their parents after school. That usually solved the problem. When I was a kid in school (and I was no 'angel either, sometimes!), the worst thing that I feared was the idea that one of my teachers was going to telephone my parents! So if I was misbehaving or disrespectful, and the teacher threatened to call my parents, I quickly shut up!

One day a kid in my seventh grade class was acting out. I threatened to call his parents, but the wise-guy kept it up, acting like he didn't believe me. So I opened my roll-book, where I had everybody's name, test grades, homework grades, address, phone number, and their parent's names, looking up that information for the wise-guy kid, to let him know that I was serious! T then began to read that information from the roll-bookout loud, in front of the entire class, to convince him to shut up since I was making sure his phone number and parents' names were correct. When I reached his parents names, I noticed that his mother's name was "Mrs. Sharp-Rock". I said to him, out loud, "MRS. SHARP-ROCK? Is that REALLY your mother's name?" (His mother, remarried, so HER last name was not the same as HIS last name). Then I began to laugh, out loud! He asked me why I was laughing, and I said, again, "Mrs. SHARP-ROCK?"-- are you serious?" He said "yes", and again I started laughing! He asked me again why I was laughing, and I said, out loud, "Mrs. SHARP-ROCK??? Sounds like somebody on the FLINTSTONES!" The entire class BURST-OUT in laughter! Since that time, I never had any behavior problems with that kid! And I never DID have to call Mrs. Sharp-Rock! PROBLEM SOLVED!

THE KID WHO REFUSED TO HANDLE THE ROCK

One of the subjects I taught as a high school teacher was Earth science. Topics taught in that course were things such as weather and climate, properties of the ocean, lakes, and rivers, earthquakes and volcanoes, and astronomy, among other topics. One of the major topics taught were rocks and minerals. There are 3 kinds of rocks: igneous—formed by heat and fire, sedimentary----- formed by deposition of sediments such as sand and clay on the bottom of oceans, lakes, and rivers, and metamorphic—formed by chemical changes, heat, and/or pressure. Some examples of igneous rocks are granite, obsidian (volcanic glass), and basalt, (formed from cooled lava). Some examples of sedimentary rocks are sandstone, limestone, and shale. Some examples of metamorphic rocks are marble, slate, gneiss, and schist. For hands-on teaching, teachers would passed around actual samples of different rocks and minerals for the kids to look at, pick up, feel, and examine, in order to get them to easily identify an unknown rock or mineral by name. Teachers made sure that the kids received and handled samples of all three rock types. One day I was walking around the room, handing out samples of all 3 rock types to each student. As expected, they picked up all the rocks, handled and examined them, then tried to identify each rock they held by name.

One kid, kind of a 'wise guy' type, took his rock samples, one by one as instructed, and began naming each one. When he got to the metamorphic rocks, he did the same, but there was ONE rock he REFUSED to take, which happened to be the schist sample. I told him he had to handle EVERY rock presented to him, but he continued to REFUSE to handle the schist with no explanation. I said to him "I don't understand-

---you handled the granite, you handled the limestone, you handled the basalt, you handled the marble, you handled the gneiss----why won't you handle the schist?????". He stood up, looked me straight in the face, and replied "I don't take no SCHIST from anybody!".

"RJ---I THINK IT'S TIME FOR YOU TO GET ANOTHER DEGREE!"

My uncle Izzy was a very "down-to-earth" guy. Whenever he had an opinion about something, he let you know it! He was the superintendent of a post office branch, and ran the venue as efficiently as possible, which he prided himself in! In his later years, and many years after his retirement he was always complaining about "incompetence"! No matter what field someone was in, if uncle Izzy felt that the person didn't really know his or her job correctly, he labeled that person (or even the whole company) as "INCOMPETENT"! He always said that he never could understand how our society reached its level of greatness, when nobody seems to know what they're doing! I, admittedly, did somewhat agree with him, and I understood what he was saying and why he was saying it: he wanted things to run PERFECTLY!

Anyway, whenever I did or said something that he didn't agree with, or that he thought was stupid or foolish (like writing this BOOK!), he would say, sarcastically, "RJ---I THINK it's time for you to get "ANOTHER DEGREE!" (He was very critical of all the degrees I went to school for, and all the schools I went to, and all the TIME I spent on that). Then I would respond, "Yes, but in what SUBJECT should I get another degree in"? Then he would respond, "in STUPIDITY"! Then I would respond, "YES, but I don't know what SCHOOL to go to for that!" Then he would respond "I KNOW what school!" Then I would respond "Yeah? What School?" Then he would respond by naming one of the schools that I received a degree from. Then we'd both laugh!

"AND ME AND ALL MY PAPERS GOT SOAKING WET!!!"

When I was in graduate school (ONE of them), I was taking a lecture class which was rather small, say about 15 students, maybe even less. One day during lecture, the professor decided to tell us about an incident that occurred to him a few hours earlier. The building had 5 floors, and in between each floor were many pipes—some carried freshwater, some carried wastewater, some carried steam, etc. This means that pipes ran throughout the ceilings of each room, including the professors' personal rooms. Apparently, as my professor was busy sitting at his desk grading tests and papers, a pipe in the ceiling right above him BURST! The pipe was carrying water (I don't know if it was freshwater or wastewater---he didn't say!). He told us that he was busy grading papers, "AND A PIPE IN THE CEILING BURST, AND ALL OF A SUDDEN, the water began pouring down from the ceiling, AND ME AND ALL MY PAPERS GOT SOAKING WET!". Immediately, in my own mind, I could picture him sitting in his chair at his desk marking papers, and seeing, literally, a WATERFALL coming down on him and all his papers! I could not stop laughing! I tried to hide it as best I could, by covering my mouth, trying to stay silent! But I couldn't help it! Throughout the entire lecture, (which ran for over two hours!), I sat there, HYSTERICAL, covering my mouth and face to prevent him from seeing me laughing! I was laughing so hard I almost CHOKED! I couldn't even BREATHE—I almost SUFFOCATED! Whether he saw me laughing hysterically or not, I'll never know!

THE CASE OF THE MISSING MASTER'S DEGREE!

As I had explained previously, probably several times, I am a 'professional student', with four Master's degrees and a Ph.D. These degrees were in biology, educational administration and supervision, and school guidance and counseling. After receiving my Ph.D. in biology, I began taking graduate classes in the geosciences at a university in one of the five boroughs of New York City, but I'm not going to tell you the name of the school nor the exact location. I took these classes because in addition to my interest in the biological sciences, I was always interested in the Earth sciences as well. So for a number of years, every term, I took one or more graduate and undergraduate classes in the geosciences, as well as in other non-related subjects. Eventually, I wanted something to show for all this, so I decided to apply to the school for matriculation into their geosciences program and earn a Master's degree. After being accepted, I continued taking classes, but I was in no hurry to finish the degree, as I had no real 'need' for it anyway. I was just being a 'professional student' taking classes that I was strongly interested in! I continued taking classes term after term, and eventually felt it was time to graduate and get the additional degree. The degree required about 30 credits, but I had amassed MANY more than that, so I had to fill out and submit a request form for graduation to the administration, after which they were to check that I had met the requirements and thus they would approve the graduation request.

A few weeks later I received a letter from the administration telling me of a problem. They only allow students 7 years to complete the program, but they told me that I was in the program for more than TWENTY-ONE years! They also told me that the program required only

30 credits, and asked why I had amassed more than TWO HUNDRED!!! They asked me to explain the reason I spent so many years in the program! I explained that I was a 'professional student' and was not in any hurry for another Master's degree. Then they sent me another letter, telling me that I did not qualify for the degree because over that 21year period, the departmental degree requirements had changed! Even though the department administrators informed them, in writing, that they recommend that I be granted the degree, the graduate school administration refused; instead, they kept negotiating with me and the department, back and forth, trying to resolve the problem. The main problem was that the original requirements included the passing of a comprehensive examination, but many of my past professors who were needed to administer and grade the exam were no longer there! Some had retired, some went to other universities, and some just DIED! In addition, the department no longer even ADMININISTERS the comprehensive exams! This controversy went on and on, for over a year, and finally I just decided to FORGET about it----I didn't really need the damn degree ANYWAY! I went to another university to take classes THERE instead!

    The university that refused to grant me the degree still sends me letters, periodically (form letters disguised as personal letters), asking me to DONATE MONEY to them! YEAH----- **THEY GOT A GOOD CASE!!!!**

THE RJ APPLESEED GAME!

I am actually the inventor of a new game, which I am officially introducing herewith! We've all (or almost all) heard of "Johnny Appleseed"? Well, this game is called the "RJ Appleseed Game", (named after ME, its founder, RJ Nobleman!). Let me explain how I discovered it and how it works: As a kid, after eating an apple, I found that the seeds were very slippery and hard to keep in your hand or even between your fingertips. (By the way, you should NEVER eat apple seeds or seeds of certain other fruits, like pears or quinces, possibly other fruits as well, because they contain cyanide, which is toxic!). Anyway, I found that if I held a seed between two fingers—the index finger and the thumb--, then squeeze, the seed will go flying very fast, like a bullet or some other type of projectile! If I pointed the seed at the wall, then squeezed it between the thumb and index finger, the seed would go flying out and hit the wall, and I would hear a "THUMP". The same would happen if I pointed the seed at the ceiling! Even better and MORE EXCITING, ----- if I pointed the seed at the venetian blinds, the "THUMP" would turn into a "PING"! (Of course, I would only do it if my parents were not at home)! If you were to get a Chinese Gong, you would get the same "THUMP", and if the going were thin enough you would hear a "PING"! So this can become a new type of GAME----competitors could take turns to see how many "THUMPS" or "PINGS" they each could get, and the winner would have gotten the most. In addition, the gong could be moved farther and farther away (almost like a limbo stick moving downward), because the farther away the gong is, the harder it is to get a hit! The one who gets the most hits win the game! You could even make DISTANCE AWAY from the gong part of the score! For example, if you get a hit ("PING") from 5 feet away from the gong, you get one point; 10 feet away---two points, 15 feet away could be three points, etc. I can foresee this game taking place at parties, family/friends 'get togethers', and even in GAMBLING CASINOS! EVEN on a TV GAME SOW! And if a Chinese gong is not available, you can do what I once did: I went to an instrumental music store and saw a cymbal on a stand for sale, and I asked the salesman if I could buy the cymbal minus the stand! Wanting to make a sale, he did just THAT! People who saw me carrying one lone cymbal out of the store began SCRATCHING THEIR HEADS!!!! But remember, I MEANT WELL! (It just doesn't always work out that way!).

"BINGO!!!"

When I was a kid, maybe 10 or 12 or so, there was a bingo hall in my neighborhood (actually several of them), where bingo games were held daily. It was usually packed with players, DOZENS of them, mainly elderly retirees. My mother and aunt liked to play bingo there often, and one day they invited me to play as well. I was sitting at a table with many other players, whom I did not know, nor did they know me (until that day, after which I'm sure they never forgot me!). At first, I was excited to play, but after a while, if I did not win, it became boring---especially for a kid!). So if I won, I would scream out, at the top of my lungs, **"BINGO!!!"**, and everybody near me would be SHOCKED, and would certainly wake up, had they been sleeping! One day, I did not win, and I wasn't even getting close, and was very bored! I happened to find an empty paper bag that someone left on the table, so, out picked it up, blew it full of air, and SLAMMED it onto the table, creating a SONIC "BOOM"! Everyone around me jumped up, out of SHOCK! Needless to say, neither my mother nor my aunt invited me to play bingo with them again!

"ECHYL-BAH-DECHYL!"

(The "Ch" sounds are soft, like you're clearing your throat, as in the word "chutzpah"). When I was a kid, my next door neighbor was a dentist, and his office was in his home. He was also MY dentist, since we were neighbors and all I had to do was literally, walk next door to his office. While he was working on my teeth, I guess he wanted to be funny and make me laugh, so he would, out of nowhere, suddenly yell out "ECHYL-BAH-DECHYL!", but he would yell it out FAST---"ECHYLBAHDECHYL!" "ECHYLBAHDECHYL!" "ECHYLBAHDECHYL!", and every time he did that, I would laugh! What that word actually meant, or what its purpose was, is beyond me! I guess it was his way of making me laugh. It reached the point where every time I saw him, whether as a patient or just on the street, I would yell out to him "ECHYLBADECHYL!" "ECHYLBADECHYL!" "ECHYLBAHDECHYL!", at which he would just ignore me. People passing by who heard me yell that out to him probably thought I was just a nutty kid (which I definitely WAS---and STILL AM as an adult!).

THE CARBON MONOXIDE DETECTOR FROM HELL!

I was driving to my friend's house. He lives in a large apartment building here in Brooklyn, about a 15-minute drive from my home. Once there I would ring his bell, and on the intercom I would tell him that I was there, then he would come down in a few minutes and meet me in the lobby. Then we would go to a nearby restaurant for dinner, using his car, so that we would not have to use separate cars. One evening, as I was approaching his home, the street was closed off. I did not know why, until I saw a squad of fire engines in front of his apartment complex. I called him on my cell phone, and told him we will be delayed because there were fire engines in front of his house! He said he didn't even know that, but he would try to find out why. After about 30 minutes, the fire engines left, and he came down to the lobby to meet me. He found out that the reason the fire department was there was that someone called 911 when their carbon monoxide detector sounded, so they had to inspect the guy's apartment to find out why it sounded and to make sure there was no carbon monoxide present. It turns out that the guy put his carbon monoxide detector on the ceiling directly above his stove, and the alarm sounded while he was cooking! (That guy must have been a real GENIUS!). Any way the fire department told the guy to move his detector to another room. After the entire scenario was over, my friend spoke to the guy and told him "Sir, excuse me, but I would like you to know that I was supposed to go to dinner almost an hour go, but because YOU called the fire department, I'm now an hour late!". The guy replied, "Yes, I understand, your dinner is more important than my LIFE! After few additional choice words between both of them, we took off to the restaurant. I guess they just don't make carbon monoxide detectors like they used to!

THE BAKERY FROM HELL

On the next block to my house, at one time there was a small grocery store and bakery (all in one) on the corner. I used to go there every morning to buy my favorite food—DOUGHNUTS--- for breakfast—usually two, three or four at a time! While there, I usually also bought a few grocery items, milk, butter, breads, and rolls of different types. The store owner, who was also the cashier, had the breads and rolls directly behind him, in baskets. So when a customer asked for breads or rolls, the owner simply turned around, and put those items in a plastic or paper bag, then added it to the other items, and rang the price of all the items up. One morning, as he was putting my rolls from the basket into the bag, one of the rolls accidently fell on the floor (obviously the guy was a real 'KLUTZ'!) Obviously, he was not about to pick up the roll from the floor and put it into MY bag, because he knew it was unsanitary, and he KNEW I was watching! So he simply left it on the floor and put a new roll into my bag. BUT……instead of picking up the roll that fell and putting it in the, trash, he picked it up from the floor and PUT IT BACK IN THE BASKET!!!! And the STUPID IDIOT DID IT RIGT IN FRONT OF ME! What a MORON!!! *I* started to laugh (after all, why should I care if someone else gets the dirty roll???....so long as it wasn't going to be ME!!!!!). To show you what an IDIOT the guy was, if I were him, I would have waited until the customer (me) left the store, and THEN I would have put the DIRTY ROLL back into the basket for the NEXT 'sucker' to buy! THAT would be what you would call "having a good head for business"!

WHY YOU SHOULD *NEVER* CHEW GUM IN CLASS!

When I was a kid in elementary school, there was always a rule that you were not allowed to chew gum in class. Some teachers said the reason was that you could not chew gum unless you have a stick of gum for every kid in the class. Some teachers didn't give a reason. My suspicion was that the teacher didn't want to feel like he or she was teaching a bunch of COWS, (even though they would probably BEHAVE better)! Be that as it may, that was the rule. If the teacher saw you chewing gum, you had to get rid of it, usually by throwing it away in the waste basket in front of the room. Most kids would first tear out a sheet of paper from their notebook, then spit the gum onto the paper or tissue like a lady or gentleman with 'CLASS', crumble it up, and drop into the waste basket. I, and a few other kids, being the 'no-class' SLOB that I was, just walked to the front of the room, looked down into the waste basket, and simply SPIT out the gum right into it! Other kids would watch and yell out "EEEEEEWWWW! EEEEEWWWW! EEEEEEEEEEWWWWWWWWWWWW!!!!" Of course, we could have just SWALLOWED the gum, but they say that wasn't healthy (possibly because if it went through your digestive system, unchanged, and if you later FARTED, you might blow a BUBBLE out of your anus, and it would destroy your underwear!!!). (Imagine trying to pull bubble gum residue off cotton!). Anyway, I used to attend an after-school class, and the teacher caught me chewing gum one day. He told me that it was against the rules and that I have to get rid of it! I told him that I didn't want to spit it out because I had just bought it a few minutes earlier, and it still had its sugar and flavor (usually the flavor and sweetness would last about half an hour).

He said he was "sorry", but the rules state that gum-chewing was not permitted in class, and that I MUST get rid of it, even if the chewing gum had NOT lost its FLAVOR yet! So---being the SLOB that I was (and still AM!), I had a better idea! I spit out the gum into my hand, and put it directly into my SHIRT POCKET! That way I could save it for later, after class. The teacher, seeing this, walked over to me, and pressed his finger, several times, onto the outside of my shirt pocket, thereby making the gum STICK to the inside of it, PERMANENTLY! The other kids laughed when they saw this, but being the SLOB that I was (and still am!), I couldn't care LESS! When I got home, I tried my best to remove as much of the gum as I could from the inside of my shirt pocket. After getting out about 50 percent of it, I simply put it back into my mouth and continued chewing, until it finally really DID lose its flavor! When my mother eventually put the shirt into the washing machine, she asked me why there was GUM in the pocket! I explained the whole story to her. Needless to say, she did not think much of that teacher, (and neither did I)!

"OHHHHHHHHH! DISSIN' THE TEACHER'S ONIONS!"

When I was teaching high school biology, every week there was one day of laboratory. One lab experiment involved looking at onion cells under the microscope. The lab technician cut onions into small pieces, and the students had to pull off a very thin piece of onion tissue, place it on a glass microscope slide, then add iodine as a stain, and observe the cells under the microscope. The technician had to cut the onion into pieces before the class started, and placed them in a small dish with some water, so that they would not dry up. The onions literally stunk to high heaven, and the students had to peel off a very thin piece of onion tissue with tweezers and their fingers! Most students did not like having to handle the onions with their fingers, but gloves were not usually provided, and their fingers wound up smelling like ONIONS for the rest of the day! I kept hearing complaints from them that the onions smelled horrible, sometimes causing their eyes to tear as well! Nevertheless, they HAD to do the experiment if they wanted to get a passing grade. Sometimes, the lab technician, instead of preparing the onion slices fresh each day, would cut them into slices only once or twice for the entire week. This produced onion slices that really STUNK! One kid, as he was taking his onion slices, said to me "Boy---these onions STINK!!!" I then said to him" OHHHHHHHHHHH! ---DISSIN' the teacher's ONIONS!". He laughed hysterically and said "Have you---have you---have you reached some kind of LOW POINT in your life?" I laughed but didn't answer him, but I WANTED to say "YEAH--the day I started TEACHING!!!"

BURNING ACES'!

Several years ago, I very STUPIDLY pulled a callus off my foot, just behind and below my big toe. This is something one should NEVER do! One should NEVER pull off a callus anywhere from their feet! Anyway, I pulled it off and it refused to heal, leaving me with a foot ulcer, which actually required dozens of visits to podiatrists and took about two years to finally heal! In that time, the open wound had gotten infected several times and required antibiotics, both oral and intravenous doses! Finally the infection required surgery, after which I had a visiting nurse show up several times a week. She wrapped the wound with an ace bandage during each visit, and told me that the bandage was washable and then re-usable, but it had to be DRY by the time she arrived. Sometimes, after I washed it, the bandage was still wet or damp before she was scheduled to arrive, so I would put it in the microwave for a minute or so, and it would soon dry out after it was removed. One day, after washing the bandage, I forgot she was scheduled to arrive soon, and the bandage was still wet or damp, so I quickly put it into the microwave and set it for a longer time---about 5 or 7 minutes instead of the usual 2 minutes, and suddenly, I smelled something funny, and the room seemed to smell horrible and the air looked 'smoky'! Then I remembered the ace bandage was in the microwave, so I ran over to take it out, and found that it had actually CAUGHT ON FIRE! I quickly put it in the sink and turned the faucet on to extinguish the flame! The bandage was DESTROYED, and the house became FULL OF SMOKE! I had to open all the windows and doors and go outside on my porch for a while until the smoke dissipated! Even after the smoke dissipated, the house smelled like BURNING RUBBER for at least an entire week! Lesson Learned: ---give washed ace bandages a few DAYS to dry out, and DO NOT PUT THEM IN THE MICROWAVE!!!

THE MOVIE PROJECTOR--------FROM HELL!

When I was teaching high school biology, teachers often showed movies to the kids. Movies make the subject more interesting (usually), and it keeps their attention, which in itself is half the battle! VCRs were not that common nor available in those days, so we often resorted to showing movies using the old-fashioned projectors with the two 'wheels' of film, one wheel fed the projector, while the other 'wheel' took up the film as the movie progressed. Then, after the movie was over, the teacher would just push a button and the wheels would spin in the opposite direction in order to rewind the film before putting it back in the 'can'; that way it can be shown again to the next class.

One day, a few minutes after the period started, I set up the projector and was ready to show the movie to the class, but when I pushed the start button, nothing happened! I kept pushing the "start" button over and over again, but it just would not start! "UH-OH!", I said to myself and the class," I think the projector's broken", figuring it was an old machine and it had just (finally) broken down. "I don't understand why this crappy projector isn't working", I told the class several times, trying to figure out what was wrong. Finally, a girl called out to me and pointed her finger towards the floor, and I found out why the projector wasn't working-----I forgot to plug it in! "OOOPS", I shouted, then plugged it into the socket and sure enough, it went on! I can't tell you how STUPID I looked, (and FELT!).

"WELL, NOW THAT SOMEBODY'S HERE, I GUESS I'LL HAVE TO WASH MY HANDS!"

We've probably all been in restaurant restrooms, and there' almost always a sign there that states "Employees must was their hands before leaving the restroom"! I've always wondered if all the employees really DO wash their hands, especially when or if there are no customers present in the restroom! (Remember the saying "if a tree falls in the forest and nobody's around to hear it, does it make noise?"). Anyway, while I was in the restroom doing my business in the urinal, a colleague entered. We were on a break and had free time, so we began to 'talk shop', 'chewing the fat', "throwing the bull"! When we were both done with our 'business' in the urinals, and as we were getting ready to leave, I said to him "Well, now that someone else is here, (meaning HIM),I guess I'll HAVE TO wash my hands!" He laughed, but I wonder if he laughed because he thought it was a joke, or because he knew it was true!

WHO'S THAT TAP-PING, AT MY SHOUL-DER?

(sung to the tune of the song "Who's That Knocking at My Door?")

I've had dogs all my life, from age 12 onward. My first dog was a mixed breed (mutt/mongrel) named "Pal". My next two dogs were Basset hounds, "Axelrod" and "Alvina", and my current dog is "Shnopsy", a Chinese Shar-Pei. Whenever I see a dog, I usually like it, especially if it seems friendly! One day, while crossing a busy street in lower Manhattan, there were many people crossing the street with me at the same time, and one guy was croissing with a beautiful yellow/golden dog, I think it was either a Golden Retriever or a Labrador. The dog was very well-behaved and crossing the street alongside is owner. I had the urge to pet it, but I chose not to do that, for two reasons (1) The owner might not like the idea, and (2) I once sometimes a dog which seems calm and friendly might not be so friendly if you touc it. (I once saw a dog in the rear of a pick-up truck which also seemed nice, calm and friendly. As I began to approach it to say "hello" and pet it, it GROWLED at me! So I began to think that petting it or even getting closer to it might not be such a good idea after all, and quickly backed away)! So, getting back to this dog that was crossing the street close to me, alongside its owner, instead of petting I, decided to just tap it, but again, I wasn't sure if the owner would like that, and I didn't know if the dog might not like it either! So, I very quickly tapped the dog on its shoulder, BUT-

---I tapped it on the shoulder on the opposite side of me, ---the side closest to its owner. After the quick shoulder tap, the dog obviously thought its OWNER tapped it, so as it continued to cross the street, it kept looking at its owner instead of me, and I could see the puzzled expression on the dog's face, as if to say "Master, why did you tap me? What do you want?" The owner was oblivious to the whole thing, not even knowing what just happened! Not so for the dog---- it kept looking at is master, WONDERING why he tapped it. Whether the dog ever figured out that is was ME, rather than his master who tapped him, I'll never know! It will just have to remain one of those 'UNSOLVED MYSTERIES'!

"AN OLD BAG!"

When I was teaching high school, one day during the changing of classes, as I was passing through the halls to my next class, I noticed a student and a teacher in conversation, apparently arguing with each oter. Being the YENTER (nosybody) that I was (and still AM), I wanted o know what the argument was about, but I had to do it in a subtle way, not to be noticed eavesdropping! I did not recognize the student, because I had not had him in my classes before, but the teacher was a veteran teacher, an 'old-timer', who had been in the school for many years before me, and he had a 'not-so-friendly ' personality (not exactly "Mister Congeniality"!) I'll call him "Mr. Pinetree". I heard the student say something like "Well, I'm going to tell my grandmother about this". Then the teacer said "I've told you OVER and OVER and OVER again, I don't want to hear ANYTHING about your GRANDMOTHER!". Then I continued walking to my next class, not knowing how the conversation ensued. A few months later, when the next term started (the school year had two terms), I had a student in my class who I did not recognize, as he was never in my class before. He was not a 'bad' kid, but a little 'off', if you know what I mean. But he did fairly well on his tests, so I gave him passing grades, which he deserved. Apparently, his guardian was his grandmother. One day in class, he told me that Mr. Pinetree had failed him the previous term, so he was not exactly a 'fan' of Mr. Pinetree! As we got to talk, he told me that one of the reasons he did not get along with Mr. Pinetree was that Mr. Pinetree called his grandmother an "OLD BAG"! I know what Mr. Pinetree's personality was like, so I definitely DO believe he called the kid's grandmother an "OLD BAG", because he said things like that not only to kids but to other teachers as well! Then I asked the kid "OH! Were you the kid who was arguing with Mr. Pinetree last term in the hall, when he said he didn't want to hear ANYTHING about your GRANDMOTHER"? He said, "YES, that was me!" I asked what the argument was about, and he responded that his grandmother had come up to school several times, and spoke to Mr. Pinetree about his attitude toward him, so he told Mr. Pinetree that he was going to report him again to his grandmother, and Mr. Pinetree said ""I told you OVER and OVER and OVER again, I don't want to hear ANYTHING about your GRANDMOTHER---she's an OLD BAG!"

I'm sure most people you would tell this story to would never believe it----that you were exaggerating---that a teacher would NEVER say such a thing to a student! But, if I know Mr. Pinetree, I'd bet MONEY that that was EXACTLY what he said! And the SAD thing about it was, he usually got away with it!

DAY CAMP SONATAS!

When I was a kid, starting around age 9 or so, my parents sent me to day camp during the summer vacations (I wonder WHY! ---probably to get me out of their hair for a few hours each day!). There were a few local day camps in the area). These day camps were held at local high schools which during the summer vacation months were used as day camps. The local day camps in my area (central Brooklyn) were held at Lafayette high school and New Utrecht high school. They would pick the kids up at selected stops in these yellow school buses, the kind we now call "cheese buses". Then they brought us to the camp, and in the afternoon, around 4 o'clock, they would bring us back home, dropping us off at the same locations where they picked us up in the morning. There was always a rivalry between the kids who went to the Lafayette day camp and those who went to the New Utrecht day camp. The kids who went to New Utrecht camp would shout things at the buses that brought kids to Lafayette camp, and vice-versa. The kids who went to the New Utrecht camp would call the Layette camp "LOUSY-ETTE", instead of "Lafayette", and the Lafayette kids would call the New Utrecht kids other names, of which I have now forgotten. When buses passed each other, the New Utrecht kids would yell out the windows "WE HATE LOUSY-ETTE! WE HATE LOUSY-ETTE!" while the Lafayette kids would yell out "WE HATE NEW UTRECT! WE HATE NEW UTRECHT!" Eventually the New Utrecht kids made up a song, I don't remember all the lyrics, but part of it was "……We'll BEAT You IN, We'll BEAT you OUT, We'll fill your mouths with SAU-er-KRAUT! HAIL! HAIL! the GARBAGE PAIL and you're welcome to LOUSY-ETTE!". And I'm sure the Lafayette kids had a song as well, for the New Utrecht kids, but since I spent most of my summers at New Utrecht, I don't remember THEIR song!

"MAKE SURE YOU EAT THE CREAM!"

I and a friend often go to a function in the mornings, and the group serves coffee and various pastries, cakes and donuts. Often, there are extras which we take home, rather than have them left over and getting stale going to waste. My friend told me that he took home a type of pastry one day---it was a rich, chocolate devil's food cake, in the shape of a pyramid, with a thick chocolate covering and creamy stuff inside. He told me that when he took it home and began to eat it, his wife yelled at him because it was unhealthy. She said it was loaded with sugar, and the creamy material inside was loaded with saturated fat and who knows WHAT else! Actually, I'm sure she was right---she was just looking out for his health! I told him, jokingly, next time to break the pastry open, then get a spoon, then scoop out the cream in front of her, and throw all the other parts away, and just eat the CREAM! A few days later, that kind of pastry was left over again, and he was wrapping it up to take it home. When I saw that, I told him take it home and eat it at home, but to make sure he eats the cream! Then I told him to eat it only in FRONT of his WIFE! Then I told him to tell her that "RJ told me to do that!". Whether he actually did that or not is a good question!

"rrrrrrrrrrrrrrRIPPPPPPPP!" and 'SPIDER MAN'!

While I was going no college, I worked part time for a company that was run by two brothers, who, let's just say, didn't always quite get along with each other. One brother who I will call Gary, was previously an engineer, and every time he watched me working, he always had a 'better version' of how to do the job, to the point where he became ANNOYING! One day he was repairing a machine, and being an engineer, and someone who always 'had a better way of doing things' one would think that he knew all the 'ins' and 'outs' of whatever repairs were needed. As he was perfecting his project, and was walking around the machine, all of a sudden I hear "rrrrrrrrrrrrrrrrRIPPPPPPPP"! Wondering what that strange noise was, I immediately looked his way, and noticed that he RIPPED his PANTS on the side of the machine! I was HYSTERICAL, and still am so to THIS DAY, whenever I think of that incident! And to make the matter worse, the pants he ripped were not old work jeans—they were expensive dress pants! Boy, that really MADE MY DAY!

On another occasion, this same former engineer pulled what I would call a 'Spider-Man' stunt! In that company, there were four floors, but no elevator. When things had to be brought to a higher or lower floor, we had to use either a dumb waiter or an electric-powered hoist, which was no more than a strong wire, thick steel hook, and thick rope that would wrap around the item to be hoisted. Every time I operated the hoist, Gary, the former engineer, would come by and show me his 'improved' method of sending things up and down. One would think his expertise as a former engineer would really make a difference in completing the task successfully! YES! It sure did. While he was sending a heavy load of materials down from the second floor to the first (ground) floor, all of a sudden I hear him SCREAM out "LOOK OUT!" then a CRASH! The rope slipped off the heavy load, CRASHING to the floor! And a couple of seconds later, GARY came tumbling after (like HUMPTY DUMPTY)! It was like watching an episode of "SPIDER MAN"! He wasn't badly hurt, but I suppose his EGO as the ENGINEER HOIST EXPERT was damaged!

THE ORANGE CONSPIRACY!

When I was in college, I worked part-time for a tobacco company in Manhattan, where they imported cigarettes, cigars, and pipe tobaccos from all over the world. I became friendly with the bookkeeper there, a mature aged woman who was friendly and conversed with me often about a variety of topics. Every year, in January, at the Fall semester's end, I visited my aunt and uncle in Florida for a couple of weeks, and before I left, I would mention it to the bookkeeper, who wished me a good time. One year, I forgot to mention to the bookkeeper that I was going back to Florida, and when I returned she was extremely angry as to why I hadn't told her about my pending trip. I really didn't have an excuse, so I apologized to her, but I told her that I did not forget her, and while I was in Florida, I DID think of her, and actually brought back a dozen oranges for her, which I had picked right off a tree in my aunt and uncle's back yard! I told her I had the oranges at home, and would bring them to her the very next day. That was a complete and total LIE! I did NOT bring her back oranges from the tree in my aunt and uncle's back yard---in fact, my aunt and uncle didn't even HAVE an orange tree in their back yard! In fact, they didn't even HAVE a back yard, because they lived in a condo! But I had to make up at least SOME kind of story just to pacify her! So the very next day, on my way to work, before I reached the subway station, I stopped by a local fruit store and bought her a dozen very big, very sweet oranges (I think they were large Mineolas---the kind with the 'bump' on top). I had to examine the oranges very carefully to make sure there was no kind of brand-name ink mark on them, so that she would not know they were store-bought oranges! Then, when I arrived at work, I gave them to her, and she thanked me without end! I told her, "see, I forgot to tell you that I was going o

Florida, but I really DID think of you when I was there by bringing you these oranges which I PERSONALLY picked off my aunt and uncle's tree!" Boy, she was really happy to hear that! The next day at work, she kept thanking me again and again! She said "Thanks a MILLION for those DELICIOUS oranges! You know, you can really TELL when they are picked right off the tree!". I just stood there and smiled!

"YOU MIGHT AS WELL HAND OUT POPCORN"!

When I was teaching science to my high school classes, I often brought in movies about science, as it seems to get the kids' interest. This was before the school had the budget to purchase VCR's, so we usually had to use those old reel-to-reel projectors, the kind that you have to rewind after the movie was finished. Now they're probably considered ANTIQUES! Anyway, one day my supervisor came in the room while I was showing the movie to ask me a question (probably some trivial, and as usual, non-sensical matter), and while I was answering his question, the movie ended (the movies usually lasted only about 15 minutes or so). So I told the kids, in front of him "OK—let me rewind this movie and then I'll put on the second movie". At the end of the period, my supervisor met me in the hallway and told me, quietly, that it was "not academically sound to show movies for 40 minutes!" I told him that these movies were about the topic we were currently covering in class. Again, he said, quietly, "It's NOT academically SOUND to show movies for 40 minutes, regardless of the topic! You might as well hand out POPCORN!". I had to cut out showing movies thereafter, because the school did not have any popcorn machines!

LEFT WITH EGG ON HER FACE!

As a final story, I'd like to introduce you to my newest dog, "Shnopsy", a female gray/blue Chinese Shar-Pei! Shnopsy is quite a character, who behaves a lot like me (RJ) when I was a kid! Shnopsy has a habit of sticking her entire face directly into the food bowl, winding up with food all over her face! Below is a picture of Shnopsy after eating a bowl of mashed hard-boiled eggs. She is always left with egg on her face, as can be seen below! (But, as always, and as the saying goes, **SHE *MEANT* WELL**! (AND SO DID I)!!!

CONCLUDING REMARKS 2

Well, you've now read more crazy but true stories that I've experienced or have been involved in. I think you're now convinced that as a kid, I really was a true "Dennis the Menace"! Now, I'm STILL a "Dennis the Menace", but as an adult rather than as a kid! Again, these stories are all true, but in some of them I had to change names in order to 'protect the innocent' (and/or THE GUILTY)! Are these ALL the stories that I have to tell? Certainly NOT! But if you want to hear more of them, you'll have to wait for the next edition----the sequel!

What's great about this book is that one does not have to read the entire book at once. You can read a few stories at your convenience, and after gaining back your composure, you can continue the readings at any time! If you wish to send me comments or questions about any of the stories, please feel free to e-mail me at:

RJNobleman@aol.com---your thoughts and comments will be appreciated, GOOD or BAD! Because even if they're bad, that means that people have actually READ the book! Well, -----thanks for reading!!!!

RJN, Brooklyn, New York, February, 2024.

www.ingramcontent.com/pod-product-compliance
Lightning Source LLC
LaVergne TN
LVHW021233080526
838199LV00088B/4331